THE EVOLUTION OF CRISES AND UNDERDEVELOPMENT IN AFRICA

Christopher E. S. Warburton

University Press of America,® Inc.
Lanham · Boulder · New York · Toronto · Oxford

University Press of America,® Inc.
4501 Forbes Boulevard
Suite 200
Lanham, Maryland 20706
UPA Acquisitions Department (301) 459-3366

PO Box 317
Oxford
OX2 9RU, UK

Printed in the United States of America
British Library Cataloging in Publication Information Available

Library of Congress Control Number: 2005924859
ISBN 0-7618-3207-6 (clothbound : alk. ppr.)
ISBN 0-7618-3208-4 (paperback : alk. ppr.)

™ The paper used in this publication meets the minimum requirements of American National Standard for Information Sciences—Permanence of Paper for Printed Library Materials, ANSI Z39.48—1984

To

My Family: Conrad, Denise, & Nabia

TUNISIA
MOROCCO
ALGERIA
LIBYA
EGYPT
WESTERN SAHARA
MAURITANIA
MALI
NIGER
CHAD
SUDAN
ERITREA
DJIBOUTI
SENEGAL
GAMBIA
GUINEA BISSAU
GUINEA
BURKINA FASO
NIGERIA
ETHIOPIA
SOMALIA
SIERRA LEONE
LIBERIA
COTE D'IVOIRE
GHANA
CENTRAL AFRICAN REPUBLIC
CAMEROON
GHANA
TOGO
UGANDA
KENYA
GABON
CONGO
DEMOCRATIC REPUBLIC OF THE CONGO
RWANDA
TANZANIA
BURUNDI
ANGOLA
COMOROS
MOZAMBIQUE
ZAMBIA
ZIMBABWE
MALAWI
MADAGASCAR
NAMIBIA
BOTSWANA
SWAZILAND
SOUTH AFRICA
LESOTHO

Contents

Foreword

This book makes a strong attempt at addressing the paradox of why so many African countries, though rich in natural resources, experienced economic hardship during the colonial era and continue to do so in decades of post-colonialism and under a variety of political regimes and economic philosophies.

The author – Christopher E. S. Warburton – expertly uses his unique academic backgrounds in history, international politics and economics in detailing and analyzing the historical, political, and economic events locally and globally that have contributed to the present state of economic affairs in the African continent.

This book, more specifically, appraises the contributions of self-serving colonial regimes and traditional authorities, corrupt and dictatorial post-colonial governments, and the lack of sound economic planning toward the social and political crises and underdevelopment experienced currently evident in a number of African states.

This masterpiece complements another book by Warburton–*Slaves, Serfs, and Workers: Labor under the Law*–which addresses the global distribution of power and its effects on our present day society.

The Evolution of Crises and Underdevelopment in Africa is a must-read for history, political, and economic scholars who are interested in the intricate combination of factors that have contributed toward the current state of political and economic affairs in Africa.

Malcolm Finney, Ph.D
California State University

Introduction

The issue of underdevelopment in Africa is a perplexing quandary, which spans several generations and several personalities. There seems to be no isolated answer to the question of African underdevelopment, but the explanations could be sought from within three significant historical experiences: (i) colonialism; (ii) failed post colonial states; and (iii) a debt crisis.

These experiences, to the best of my knowledge, have not been comprehensively treated elsewhere in the way they are presented in this work as a composite whole for the understanding of the crises in Africa. The evolution has received very little attention, unlike isolated occurrences of wars or genocide, corruption, and debt. Belatedly, some efforts have been directed to the failed state, and colonialism is occasionally seen as an issue of a bygone era. Meanwhile some African nations have spent too many resources and time trying to resolve the unsettled issues of the late 1950s and 1960s.

In reality, when the three historical experiences are juxtaposed, one is not exclusive of the others. For a very long period of time, the problems of the crisis-ridden African states were perceived by some international organizations in economic rather than in political terms, and by so doing, there was an overemphasis on economic policies rather than on political policies. The diagnoses for the problems have proven to be misguided, and the continent has registered no significant development. Fortunately, in the belated space of time, the focus is shifting to some of the major root causes of African underdevelopment—oppressive regimes, corruption, and international complicity. Four issues are, therefore, key to understanding the evolution of underdevelopment in Africa: (i) the making of the contemporary African states; (ii) the perception that political authority is economic entitlement; (iii) the theory that ethnic and other social differences are power reinforcing, belief in which results in alienation and loss of hope; and (iv) the tacit recognition of illegitimate regimes in the name of national self-determination and *sovereignty*, or international law.

The modern African state is a superstructure, which disfigured the foundation of valuable communal values. The redefining of the African concept of political organization and authority, which came with modernization, was a revolutionary endeavor, not so much for sustaining the ties with western civilization, or even friendship but for redefining territorial boundaries, and unifying social organizations into modern states based on the European perception of statehood. Ironically, the Africans were less unified on the issue but most opted for the European version of unification anyway. In British Africa, colonies and protectorates became one after independence although they were once governed as distinct or separate entities.

It could be recalled that in the seventeenth and eighteenth centuries Europeans wrestled with the concept of the modern state for reasons that might also have been apparent in Africa. The Treaty of Berlin (1885), in many ways, was to ultimately do for Africa what the Treaty of Westphalia (1648) had done for Europe.

The Treaty of Westphalia was obviously more complicated, but, like the Treaty of Berlin, it delineated frontiers for ownership and conferred sovereign rights. Sovereign rights, as defined by the Treaty of Berlin, were then passed on to the Africans for the construction of the modern states. The way Africans had to deal with the post Berlin settlement eventually became reminiscent of the pre-Westphalia European problems. Evidently, the Treaty of Berlin was inadequate simply because it was urgently intended to avoid European conflict in Africa by defining and legitimizing larger spheres of influence without consideration of the micro-problems associated with the new acquisitions.

African intellectuals obviously understood, then and now, what was a major challenge ahead—dealing with the concept of the modern democratic state and making the new superstructure amenable to the diverse needs of Africans. In actual fact, except for its modern sophistication, the essence of the present state lacks any meaningful variation from what had hitherto existed.

Since ancient times, there have been obvious philosophical differences about how the state should be configured. For example, Plato (c.427-347 BC), Aristotle (384-322 BC), Cicero (106-43 BC), Machiavelli (1469-1527), Hobbes (1588-1679), Locke (1632-1704), Rousseau (1712-78), Hegel (1770-1831), and Marx (1818-1883) had various views about the state. But, in essence, the common denominators show that all states must have a political organization or institution, which must be able to defend the citizenry from external aggression, resolve internal contradictions to maintain stability, ensure effective and unbiased distributive policies, and provide a mechanism for an orderly transfer of power.

The inability of a government to ensure the attainment of the common denominators calls into question the legitimacy and efficacy of that government. A government that has failed must then relinquish its claim to authority or allow its citizens to determine its usefulness.

Apparently, while more civilized societies use elections as a vote of confidence or a show of repugnance or failure of a political administration, most African states are yet to come to terms with the idea that elections must express a vote of confidence in government, or displeasure with political regimes. African democracy in some parts of the continent suggests that African leaders adopt an all-knowing attitude and use brute force to subdue opponents, who, for lack of a better term, engage in "treasonable activities."

What really destroyed the path to development in some African countries? The answer could be sought from conflict mismanagement and distributive injustice, which spans more than four decades of misrule. In Chapter one I show how the so-called "primitive societies" (state and stateless) were able to manage conflicts that are now consuming the modern African states.[1] The conditions for leadership were spelled out and known; the obligations of rulers and the ruled were known; rulers could be removed from office to safeguard the welfare of the commonwealth; and, in less formal societies, there were inherited aphorisms and codes of conduct for stability. This must be understood in distinction to the organization that supplanted the old form of social organization.

Chapter two shows why the construction of the new African states was problematic for a variety of reasons, including the haste with which the states were created and the principles that were utilized in creating the states. These principles have ramifications for subsequent development.

Four major powers were partly responsible for the creation of the modern African states: Britain, Germany, France, and Belgium. I revisit the policies and principles that were utilized by the British, the French, and the Belgians. This was the period of colonialism proper—a period that was characterized by political turbulence and confrontation. It was a time of division, suspicion, and conflicts not only between Africans and the imperialists, but also among Africans. The seeds of discord and chaos were planted and neither the imperialists nor the Africans had a ready solution to the problems. The basis of underdevelopment was laid not because of integration into the global capitalist market, as it is normally alleged in some literature (the new imperialist/dependency variety), but because of the inability of Africans to manage internal conflicts or disagreement and set up accountable systems to promote growth and development.

Indeed, the claim of the new African élites was that they could restore order, develop nationalism (which some believed already existed in their respective nations), and foster growth and development. Amidst the disagreements of sound political policies, fractured ethnic relations, and a precarious sense of civic responsibility or political culture, the new African élites conjured up a sense of nationalism, and sought independence for disingenuous reasons.

The adoption of western political ideas and fresh opportunities for acquiring wealth and power provided opportunities for the emergence of illegitimate regimes, which had been reinforced by coercive methods and an appeal to ethnic or parochial differences (an aberration of the western systems they were supposed to emulate). The leaders of the new and problematic African nations saw their new acquisition of power as lifelong political and economic entitlements and dared opponents to challenge that perception. Modernity came with all its niceties and conveniences as well as its discontents.

The resolution of the political leaders to stay in power has been exacerbated by the desire to amass ill-gotten wealth from the trade of valuable economic resources. These seductive resources not only strengthen the resolve of rulers to stay in power but also fuel the audacity of individuals to confront corrupt governments head on. This bravado is normally given external assistance for a stake in the wealth of nations in conflict.

Chapter three deals with the post-colonial regimes and their *modus operandi*. The post colonial regimes developed blatantly apologetic philosophical ideas for the systems they constructed—*African Democracy*, *Democratic Socialism*, or the *Peoples Democratic Republic of*... The new concepts more often than not insinuate that democracy in Africa should be different from democracy or socialism elsewhere in the world. These revolutionary concepts, which are in reality worthless political theories, have been surreptitiously used to justify the longevity of post-colonial regimes; when used contemporaneously, they do not serve any meaningful purpose.

The post-colonial regimes have also sought accessories for survival; ethnicity and religious differences. Although ethnicity (shared tribal affinities and traditions), religion, and politics are timeless aspects of the human experience, obvious differences in perception of their use have become the tools for carnage and self-destruction of some African societies. African societies have witnessed a remarkable cultural transition, which has spanned the era of trade wars, religious wars, the making of kingdoms, and the adoption of western political ideas. At no time, however, have ethnic and religious differences been used to such an extent for a few to sustain political and economic power as in contemporary African politics.[2] The struggle for political power or the insurance of it seldom leaves out ethnic or religious considerations. The net result, of course, is nepotism, grafting, favoritism, corruption, and wars. When regimes become sufficiently corrupt and oppressive, sporadic upheaval and military *coups d'état* become the immediate remedial methods for a change of regime. These methods are not always used without considerable loss of lives.

Coups d'état, which normally purport to change illicit regimes, seldom show any departure from the ways of the supplanted old regime. Army generals, corporals, lieutenants, and brigadiers embellish the post colonial lexicon of *African Democracy* with *Revolutionary*..., *Revolutionary Front, and The People's Revolutionary Council*. The word "revolutionary" has become a familiar surrogate for the so-called "deposed democratic regimes." In theory, the *coups* are clearly intended to show complete change or radical departure from the old ways of doing things in order to legitimize the seizure of power. But seizure of political power normally falls short of the expectations to bring forth the much-needed change in African politics.

Until the East Asian miracle, the failed state dressed itself in the cloak of neo-imperialism. The issue of whether underdevelopment is attributable to failed post-colonial policy or colonialism is also addressed in Chapter 3. The post-colonial policy in the featured African states is compared to policies undertaken by the Singaporean government in the immediate post colonial period; what Rostow would describe in terms of the conditions for "take-off."

In chapter 4, the real consequences of failed policies in Africa are presented. The net result of failed policies is underdevelopment—the pitiful situation which now overwhelms some of the African nations in the most dreadful terms. Underdevelopment is a measure of well being that includes a variety of indicators; the principal ones being poverty, health, education, income and income inequity, food availability, and consumption of goods and services. African underdevelopment is largely the product of more than forty years of oppressive misrule, the lack of investment in human capital and technology, the failure of governments to decentralize (rather than consolidate) political power, the general reluctance to provide or promote benevolent social programs, widespread corruption, debts (contracted by fraudulent regimes with complicit foreign nations or institutions), population growth, the unfortunate incidence of Acquired Immune Deficiency Syndrome (AIDS), and the wars which have emerged as a remedy to perceived injustice or deprivation.

It becomes puzzling to envisage whether sustainable development is an option for the African countries which are severely indebted or poor. Can these countries meet current consumption after wasting and degrading the environment with no significant traces of development to begin with? Would future generations be equally better-off or worse-off? The prospects are not very optimistic. Sustainability would require a collective effort to salvage the environment and maintain a stable level of consumption into the future. Its success would be highly contingent on how much weight is given to the socio-political conditions within the African countries, particularly the creation of a civic culture of an orderly transfer of power, which has been missing for a very long time in some African states—in short the political accountability of rulers for their policies and actions when they are not improving the general welfare.

In Chapter 5, the issues of international law, sovereign debt, and international culpability for odious debts are discussed. It is fairly reasonable to advance the argument that a multilateral convention against domestic and international corruption will minimize the level of odious debts and improve the prospects of development for the poor nations which have been the victims of fraudulent regimes. The problem is that the state is persistent and contracts made by preceding governments have been found to be binding on succeeding governments, the governments being a segment of the state.

This chapter presents the view that international law has not provided sufficient avenues for the redress of hateful debts, and that the heavily indebted countries could not really find salvation in international law for the debt crisis just now. The various methods and forums for dealing with the debt problems are discussed in the light of how they have been used in the past and the prospects they provide for resolving disputes involving sovereign debts in the future. Special emphasis is placed on the role of treaties, custom, and arbitration. Judicial settlement in the International Court of Justice (ICJ) is unlikely because of the nature of debt contracts, and the inclination of debtors to prefer rescheduling of debts for better or worse. The way and manner in which the Court could be instrumental to resolving the controversy and the principles upon which the court could arrive at its decisions are discussed.

The poor countries are not well placed to benefit from any repudiation or judicious settlement because of their incapacity to finance their development without foreign assistance (which is more often than not coordinated) and the likelihood of retaliation from creditors. I advance the view in this chapter that the remedy to the debt crisis rests more on equity and ethics rather than international law in the absence of a multilateral treaty or significant amount of bilateral treaties. The problem of African debt is not likely to be resolved or minimized in the future except by some commitment to the ratification of a convention that would forestall the preservation of odious debts. This would be one step forward to promoting African development in the future.

CHAPTER 1

THE OLD PERCEPTION OF STATE AND SOCIETY IN AFRICA

Pre-Colonial Societies of West Africa

Ghana

The notion of divine rights of kings, and/or god-fearing rulers, has been an age-old concept of wide appeal around the globe. It is supposed to espouse the judicious use of power through the will and fear of God. Without justifying or repudiating it, it is readily apparent that this doctrine is not necessarily a precondition for good behavior or benevolent rule. In actual fact, the kingdom of Ghana on the west coast of Africa resisted Islamic religious incursions for quite some time and was able to develop a remarkable political system which predates an Islamic take over.

Prior to their conversion to Islam, the Berbers, who were primarily nomadic people, formed a new kingdom called Ghana in the fifth century. It was one of the first kingdoms to be established on the west coast of Africa. The largest African cities and kingdoms were to be found in the Sahel, a desert and savannah region south of the Sahara. The emergence of cities and kingdoms could largely be attributed to trade across the desert—a north-west nexus of trade routes. Although the Berbers had started to convert to Islam during the eleventh century, it took the Islamic Berbers (the Almoravids) several years to subjugate Ghana and establish a theocracy.

One of the kingdoms that developed much later after the Islamic incursions and was able to exist for a long period of time was that of the *Ashanti*. The *Ashanti* people, who occupied what is now southern Ghana in the 18th and 19th centuries, were able to establish their power after a process of expansion, which started in 1670 under their King Osei Tutu. By 1800 the *Ashanti* Empire had become an example of a strong centralized state, with an administration based on merit. The *Ashanti* perfected the art of integrating societies into a strong state by using a sense of nationalism and diplomacy.

Osei Tutu was the fourth ruler in *Ashanti* royal history. The *Ashanti* consists of the largest contingent of the *Akan* speaking matrilineal (inheritance or succession through a mother) peoples who were formed into several clans by the middle of the sixteenth century.[3] Rather than using the now familiar principle of "divide and conquer" to maintain hegemony over the various clans, Osei Tutu sought ways to create an *Ashanti* union.

The creation of the union was an elaborate and painstaking process that involved a symbol of leadership and union, the Golden Stool. This stool is believed to have been invoked by Okomfo Anokye—the fetish priest of Osei Tutu. The stool had a religious and political essence, which represented the authority of the king and a compelling religious submission to his will, which came from a supreme being. The stool symbolized the strength of the union, only to be occupied by the king who became known as the *Ashantihene*.

As time passed by, the Golden Stool obtained progressive importance. The *Ashanti* King was very powerful, as symbolized by the *Stool*, but at the same time subservient. Western European political philosophy of the eighteenth century recognized the concept as "sovereignty of the people." The *Ashanti* King was definitely not almighty. He ruled with a council and was obligated to listen to the wishes of the council. In 1896, for example, rather than risk losing the *Stool* in a war, the *Ashantihene*, Prempeh I, went into exile. For the King's tenure of office, however, the *Stool* performed an important role.

As an annual show of strength and unity, all member states of the union attended the *Odwira Festival,* which was established as an annual reminder and reaffirmation of the unity of the nation. The union functioned with a constitution, and kings of the states of the union formed a confederacy. Although the *Ashanti* defeated a British force in 1824, their empire was eventually subjugated and annexed in 1901 by the Gold Coast Colony.

Nigeria

Centralized and decentralized states were also found in pre-colonial Nigeria. Some of the more centralized states included *Oyo*, *Kanem-Borno*, and *Gobir*. Less centralized ones included *Igbo*, *Isoko*, and *Ibibio*.

Kingdoms and Empires of Old Africa

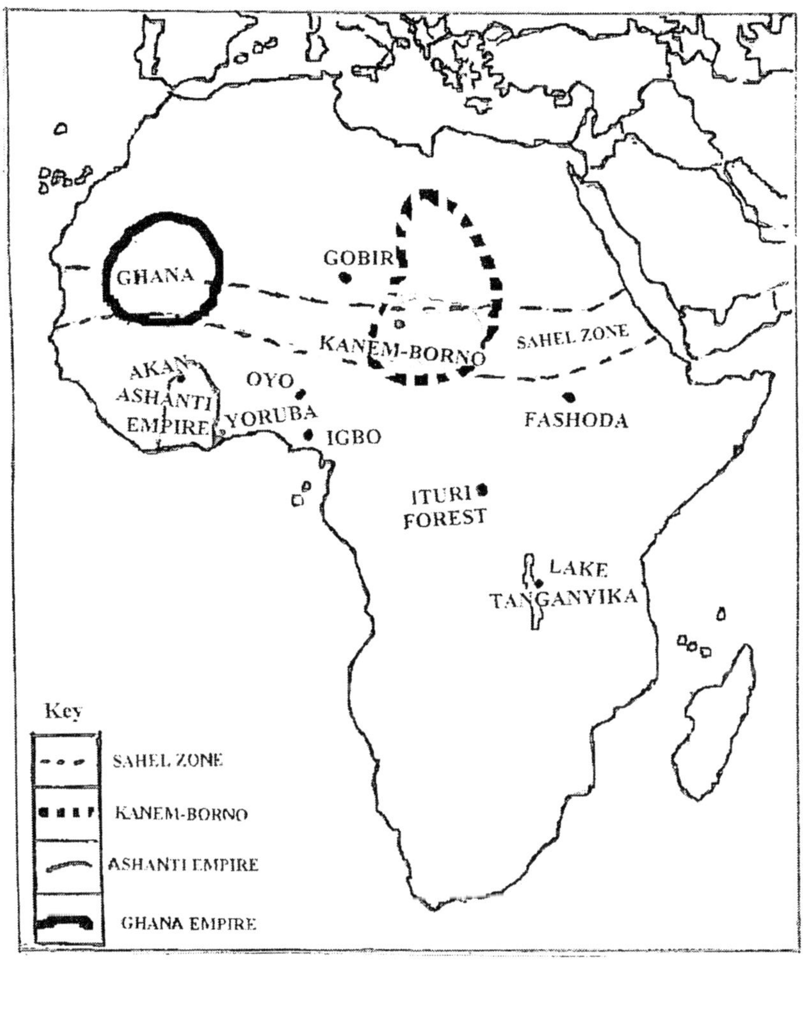

The *Oyo* Empire was a powerful *Yoruba* empire that developed in South Western Nigeria. Oral tradition suggests that the progenitor of the *Yoruba* people, Oduduwa, descended from heaven (believed to be the ancient city of Mecca in some circles) to *Ile-Ife* (*Ife*). *Ife* was the first of the medieval *Yoruba* cities. It prided itself on being a sacred city, a place where the gods descend to earth. Also, the *Yorubas* believed that they were chosen by God (*Olorun Olodumare*). Associating the primogeniture of a particular group with a deity or supernatural force is a common African disposition. Other examples included the *Mendes*, the *Nuer*, and the *Pygmies*. *Oyo* eventually succeeded *Ife* as the center of *Yoruba* life and the early rulers of *Oyo* laid the basis for what was to become an effective monarchical system.

At the center of its ascendancy was the *Alafin* (the ruler), who ruled as a semi-divine king. The *Alafin* was represented by a priest in each town. The sub-rulers of the *Alafin* constituted a council of nobles (*Oyo Mesi*), which performed judicial functions and mediated disputes between the *Alafin* and subordinate rulers. The council of nobles appointed army officers, and the *Alafin* submitted his decisions to the council for vetting. The *Oyo Mesi* could condemn an *Alafin* to death by suicide because of failure, incompetence, or inefficiency. For example, by the end of the eighteenth century, it took two months for *Maku* to be removed from office after *Adebo's* death.[4] It would be recalled that the *Ashantis* were equally capable of getting rid of the *Ashantihene* to protect their society or the Golden Stool.

The *Oyo Mesi,* in turn, was checked by notables of prominent or great families. This structure was a safeguard against royal tyranny or the excessive use of authority. A slight variation of this practice is popularly known as *checks and balances* today. It was not extraordinary for an *Alafin* to be deposed or forced to commit suicide for failure, incompetence or inefficiency.

For the *Yorubas* the link between religion and political authority was real. Even with all the divinity, awe and power, that could be associated with religion, the *Yorubas* were not willing to sacrifice belief for tyranny. Tradition holds that the fourth *Yoruba* king/*Alafin* of *Oyo*, *Shango*, came at a time of moral decay or degeneration. It was therefore necessary to restore a bygone era of rectitude by drastic means. *Olorun* had to be appeased by the renunciation of immoral turpitude, which necessitated drastic therapeutic rule.

Shango was confronted with the challenge of restoring the required moral sense. Theft was just one of those cursed crimes for which *Shango* would ask God to command thunder to strike the perpetrator. The frequency of drastic punishment earned *Shango* the name, the "Lord of Thunder." However, tradition suggests that the *Yoruba* people grew weary of drastic rule even in the name of religion.

The mysticism associated with *Shango* is comparable to that of the *Ashantihene*, and in a similar way, the rule and theories of *Shango* fostered a sense of unity among the *Yorubas*. The support of the *Shango* tradition was crucial to the success of subsequent *Alafins* and the *Oyo* Empire.[5] The basis of loyalty to the *Alafin* was established. It is believed that *Oyo* reached its peak around 1650, exercising great authority over the area between the Volta and Niger rivers.

The much less centralized society of the *Igbos* in Southeastern Nigeria was equally able to balance political authority. The *Igbos* occupied several villages and used the villages to constitute political administration. The basic political unit was therefore the village. The political structure of the village consisted of a council of elders and a village assembly. The council included heads of family units, but provision was made for adult males to participate in the deliberations of the councils. This accommodation ensured the articulation of diverse views. Elders performed the role of arbiters or judges and decisions for conflict resolutions had to be unanimous. The councils were especially designed to cut across wealth or privilege, and age boundaries. They provided a forum for the wealthy and the poor to be heard as well as young and old. Although the process would seem cumbersome, long or tedious, it was adopted to ensure maximum political participation and conflict resolution.

There were further built-in systems for political balance. These involved the use of secret societies, as was the case with the *Mendes* of Sierra Leone, and age-set organizations. Harris defines age-set as including "young people (male and female separate), initiated at a certain age, who remained members all their lives."[6] Age-sets were organized to provide discipline among the youths, promote community service and recreation, as much as to check abusive or excessive political authority. The age-sets provided a wider coordination among villages and a strong network for effective government at the village level among the *Igbos*.

Sublime mysticism was used to settle disputes. This was done through the oracle system. The role of oracles in the quest of knowledge or solution was not peculiar to the *Igbos*. Oracles were also used in much more famous societies. Socrates, for example, once checked with the oracle at Delphi to find out who was the wisest man on earth. The *Igbos,* however, used the oracle system to settle disputes between villages when an alternative option was not chosen (for example, using elders). Harris cites the *Agbala* and *Arochuckwa* oracles as media for conflict resolution between blacksmiths, on the one hand, and traders, on the other.[7]

There is probably awareness by now that a sense of belonging and attachment to the villages would create strong ethnic ties and loyalty. This loyalty resurfaced in the *Biafra* War of the late 1960s, which led to the temporary secession of *Biafra* from the Nigerian union but its eventual defeat in the ensuing war by 1970. Indeed each and every one of the various ethnic groups of Africa glorifies its past, celebrates its achievements, affirms a common bond, and maintains a substantial amount of pride. One of the greatest challenges confronting the post colonial state is how to cut through this primordial pride in ethnicity, the inordinate sense of belonging to a group believed to be superior to all others and highly sensitive to deprivations.

Sierra Leone

Pre-colonial organization in Sierra Leone shows that the *Limbas* and the *Temnes* of Sierra Leone seem to have been in contact as far back as the 600s AD in northern Sierra Leone. These kinds of contacts made it possible for values to be shared and it is not uncommon to find similar systems of political organization like that of the *Mendes*.

Their clans share common names such as *Kargbo, Kamara,* and *Conteh*. The *Lokos*, on the other hand, are closely related to the *Mendes* and the *Gbande* in parts of Liberia. Foray suggests that the *Lokos* eventually acquired a distinct *Temne* influence.[8] This influence seems to have been fostered largely as a result of trade in the north between the two groups. There seems to have been a business relationship between the *Limbas* and the *Temnes*, the *Lokos* and the *Temnes*, and the *Lokos* and the *Mendes*.

The *Kisi* who once settled in large numbers in the Eastern province of Sierra Leone, acquired many *Mende* traits and a large number also spoke *Mende*. Other groups like the *Krim* and the *Sherbro* were also absorbed by the *Mendes*. These groups also adopted the *Mende* language.

The pre-colonial history of Sierra Leone in these formative years must be understood from two parallel perspectives—one which involved interaction (sometimes leading to war for the control of trade routes and land), and another which involved a system of government based on informal institutions, negotiations and, often times, gerontocratic.

Trade was a very important medium of contact, and, according to Kup, "trade routes ran from *Bullom*, *Temne*, *Krim* and *Vai* territory up the coastal estuaries, through northern *Temne* and *Limba* country, via *Port Loko* and *Tonko Limba* in the west, or *Bafodea* and *Bumban,* thence *Falaba* (after 1768) in the east."[9] Trade articles included sea salt, cloth, gum, palm products, timber, and Kola nuts. There were often major wars to control trade routes and commerce, for which the more strategically located *Temnes* became more vulnerable. Wars were fought after careful and methodical thought.

Early kings of Africa depended on the decisions of their councils. It was not unusual for the decisions of the councils to be at variance with the expectations of the kings with no punitive backlash. When a *Temne* king wanted to go to war,

Ethnic divisions in Sierra Leone

for example, he would gather the elders and hold his council. If the war was perceived of as unjust, or if the enemy was deemed to be invincible, the king would be told in unequivocal terms that he could not be supported, and that he should pursue peace. This practice was not peculiar to the *Temne*. Recall that the *Ashantis* exiled their king, Prempeh I, rather then lose the Golden Stool in 1896.

Power diffusion was also to be found in less centralized societies. The authority of a *Bulom/Sherbro* king of Sierra Leone, for example, was restricted by a secret society known as the *Poro*. Newton observes that the *Sherbro* people lived much in a patriarchal way, and who ever was called the King was not easily distinguished either by state or wealth from the rest.[10] The many districts of the *Sherbro* were virtually independent of each other, save that they were united by an institution which pervaded them all—the *Poro*. This institution, which was also well established among the *Mendes,* was a mystical society. The *Poro* had both legislative and executive authority. Newton writes:

> Everything belonging to the *Purrow* [Poro] is mysterious and severe, but upon the whole, it has very good effects; and as any man, whether bond or free, who will submit to be initiated into their mysteries, may be admitted of the Order, it is a kind of common Common-wealth. And, perhaps, few people enjoy more, simple, political freedom, than the inhabitants of *Sherbro*, belonging to the *Purrow* (who are not slaves)[11]

Little suggests that it is probable that among the *Mendes* individual suzerainty and local policing depended to a varying degree on the offices of the *Poro* society. "It is likely that *Poro* sanctions regulated general behavior among the earliest settlers and they were adapted to the newer political situation."[12] *Mende* chiefs did not necessarily require a military force to control a territory. Chiefs with the backing of the *Poro* could use it to control a territory more effectively.

As with the *Nuer*, kinship ties were very strong among the *Mendes*. These ties were founded on respect as well as a moral sense. The moral sense cautioned against transgressions, which came with a curse. Family ceremonies would reinforce tacit understanding of family ties to forbid poverty among family members, or the sale of family property.

Prior to the creation of the modern state, the terms "villages" and "chiefdoms" carry special connotations, as much as the ownership of property and rights. Little observes that the founder of chiefdom or a section of it acquired certain rights over it. Over time, this right translates into jurisdiction over it—a political dimension.

Succession rights were clear and the *Mende* chief was a unifier. Although women became chiefs, succession to the chieftaincy was mostly patrilineal and linked to the line of the original founder. The chief was not only expected to perform the crucial role of leadership in times of war, but he was expected to adjudicate disputes for the stability of his chiefdom. Like every contemporary executive, he was also responsible for the civil and administrative functions of his chiefdom.

To perform the role of rule adjudicator, he convened his court periodically with the assistance of the important personalities of his chiefdom, including important elders. Powerful as the chief might seem, he was regarded as a *primus inter pares* (first among equals). He was supposed to consult his Chiefdom Council or body of advisers on any matter affecting the chiefdom as a whole, and he was responsible to his chiefdom for his actions. This form of political relations between the chief executive and the citizenry in modern parlance is known as accountability, a hallmark of modern democracy.

Evidence suggests that the *Mendes* were not well disposed to tyrannical rule. This was made known at the death of a chief. On this matter, Little writes:

> When a chief died in the old days a gift of ten heads of money (i.e. slaves) was made by his family to the chiefdom to obtain their favour before appointing a new chief. Had the previous ruler been tyrannical, the amount of the gift would be larger.[13]

The disposition to be remorseful evinces a moral sense, the willingness and ability to separate right from wrong and to appeal to the community for forgiveness.

Societies in East and Central Africa

Southern Sudan

Until the much-celebrated work of Sir Edward Evans-Pritchard in the 1930s and 1940s, very little was known about the *Nuer* on a global scale. The study of Sir Evans-Prichard is important not only for inviting further studies of the *Nuer*, but also for bringing into sharper focus the social organization of the *Nuer*. The *Nuer* is particularly important for this work because of their method of conflict resolution.

The *Nuer* are a Nilotic Negro people of the upper Nile, who live in the swampy plains south of *Fashoda* and at the *Bahr-el-Ghazal* confluence. Traditionally, they are cattle herders. Oral traditions also suggest that there was a greater expansion into their current territories from 1500 to 1800 A.D. It is believed that between 1818 and 1890, the *Nuer* increased the territory under their control, so that it ranged from the west central portion of the Upper Nile Basin (Sudan) to the eastern edge of that Basin. By this expansion, the *Dinka* (and *Nuak*), who inhabited that territory, came under *Nuer* control. Expansion and combination was feasible because the *Dinka* and *Nuer* came from a common stock, speak closely-related languages, formerly occupied a common ecological zone, and share similar systems of economic production.[14]

Prior to the studies of Evans-Pritchard, traders expanded their operations into previously unexplored river systems in the 1850s and 1860s and moved into the interior of the Upper Nile Basin. During the 1840s and the 1850s, missionaries arrived in the Sudan, and made initial contacts with the *Dinka* and the *Nuer*. What seems to have caught the interests of anthropologists the most about the *Nuer* since Evans-Pritchard is the interrelationship of diverse lineages, conflict management, and their orderly behavior.

The social organization of the *Nuer* showed that the threat of violence, normally associated with anarchy and destruction, could also be used to create a sense of unity when there was the absence of formal institutions to limit personal violence. Evans-Pritchard couched this as "segmentary opposition."[15]

The method of "segmentary opposition" is based on the idea of controlling violence by recognizing the danger of an external enemy and reinforcing group identities based on segmentary lineage structure. The presence of a series of nested lineages creates a situation in which the level and size of the groups participating in a conflict is determined by the genealogical positions of the parties to a dispute. A compositional/generalization fallacy (the idea that one or two might disagree) is not assumed.

Conflict and cooperation are determined by the boundaries of lineage segments or territories associated with them. Concerted action within one group is activated when there is a dispute between one of its members and the member of an opposing group—precisely how the *Nuer* united against the neighboring *Dinka*. At a lower and personal level, the potential for concerted action led to resolution of conflict at the lower level, a micromanagement of hostilities. Apart from what might seem to be a crude form of deterrence, disputes were normally resolved by fines in the form of cattle, which was regarded as a very valuable article of trade and subsistence.

The *Nuer* had no written law, yet they were far from lawless. They evidently had a moral sense, which was manifested in their ability to distinguish right from wrong. What is wrong is not necessarily ambivalent in most societies because an infraction or the infringement of a right could be ocularly identified. It was this moral sense that directed the affairs of the *Nuer*. For example, it was known to be wrong for a *Nuer* to refuse to honor his obligations toward his kinsmen or to commit homicide.[16]

Since individual wrongs were not to be isolated, they assumed a social dimension, linking the action of an individual to a segment or kinship. This social dimension brought shame and reproach to a disreputable family, which deters that family from seeking reprisal after punishment. Howell observes that the "[s]cales of compensation for wrongs can be quoted by the older generation of *Nuer* with surprising consistency... an indication neither of rigidity of custom nor of constant application."[17]

Evans-Pritchard noted that sometimes restitution involved "blood-feuds" since that is a way to obtain reparation.[18] The fight for restitution however was the result of a breach of law. *Nuer* law could however be best be described as nascent with drawbacks in enforcement. Compensation for a wrong was usually mutually advantageous since it depended on kinship or marital ties. Other ties, like the social units concerned, were equally meaningful for compensatory rights.

How could a society minimize a pugnacious tendency? In the 1960s, the world cowered and comforted itself with the dangerous theory of Mutual Assured Destruction (MAD). MAD, for sure, eventually fell into comparative insignificance in the 1980s as Star Wars took on a new initiative. The US and Russia calculated the potential of nuclear destruction and saw the acquisition of nuclear weapons as a deterrent because of the destruction it would cause to both sides. The concept of mutual fear or destruction is a timeless one and it shaped the *Nuer* desire to avoid the self-destructive calamities of wars. Evans-Pritchard puts it otherwise:

> Fear of incurring a blood-feud is, in fact, the most important legal sanction within a tribe and the main guarantee of an individual's life and property. If a community of one tribe attempts to avenge a homicide on a community of another tribe a state of intertribal war, rather than a state of feud, ensues, and there is no way of settling the dispute by arbitration.[19]

Fights between persons of different villages were bouts of escalation for which the choice of weapon was elevated from a club, for example, to a spear. Quite apart from the scale of war or the theater of its operation, the choice of weaponry unequivocally predicted the outcome of war in terms of loss of lives. It was the *a priori* knowledge of loss of life that discouraged the rush to large-scale war against neighboring villages.

The *Leopard-Skin Chief* acted as a mediator in cases of homicide to prevent widespread blood bath in the process of avenging the homicide. According to Evans-Pritchard, the chief was considered to be sacred and blood must not be shed in his homestead. He is considered to have a sacred association with the earth, which gives him ritual powers including the power to bless or curse. Yet, this authority was used with remarkable restraint.[20]

The authority of the chief was instrumental in managing feuds, but it carried with it a political dimension. While not controlling the various groups, the chief regulated the groups principally by settling feuds. The chief had no executive or judicial authority and it was not his duty to decide on the merits of a case. Although the *Nuer* were easily incited to violence, the society was observed to be thoroughly kinship oriented and democratic with no overriding controlling authority of daily life. As with the *Mendes* of Sierra Leone, kinship ties played a very important role in the political and economic organization of the *Nuer*.

Sudan's civil war, which has lasted for over a decade, has destroyed the traditional way of life and displaced many *Nuer* to neighboring Ethiopia or places in northern Sudan, such as the capital city of Khartoum.

The *Pygmies* of Central Africa

Today, some of the *Pygmies* of Central Africa lament their predicament, as they are hunted and killed. A common complaint is that the government does not even care about these marginalized people, who have been denied voting rights, excluded from public administration, and cannot even register the births of their children. *Pygmies* live in Zaire's *Ituri* forest (*Bambuti/BaMbuti/Mbuti*), Cameroon, Gabon and South Africa. Who were the *Pygmies* and how did they live?

In Zaire, there are three main groups of *Pygmies*: the *Tswa* in the west, the *Twa* between Lake *Kivu* and Lake *Tanganyika*, and the *Mbuti* of the *Ituri* Forest. In this work, allusion is made to the *Pygmies* of the *Ituri* forest, who are normally referred to as the only true *Pygmies*, i.e., under 150 cm. in height and relatively unmixed with neighboring peoples.

The *Pygmies* did not have a codified system of law, and their political organization fell into that category of social organization classified as "stateless." They had no chiefs or formal councils of elders, believed in a forest deity, and lived in nomadic bands. In several ways, the perception of the *Pygmies* about right or wrong was not any different from that of the *Nuer*, the *Igbo* or the *Mende*. The silent code of conduct dictates that right conduct must work for the general good of society. Like every society, violations of etiquette are expected, and when they occurred, the elders of the *Pygmies* played a crucial role in resolving disputes because of experience and the wisdom that is supposed to come with age.

The elders, like European judges who followed judge-made laws or common laws, used precedents to explain what went wrong and why things went wrong. An informal consensus among the respected elders was usually the basis for decision making affecting a camp. It was not uncommon for punishment for a breach of peace to be an expulsion from a band.

The life style of the *Pygmies* necessitated a symbiotic relationship with their neighbors. The *pygmies* were largely hunter-gatherers—hunting and gathering food. This presupposed a less settled life style and a more fluid one. They, therefore, needed to exchange meat and honey for cultivated products. This interdependent life-style was, in actual fact, not peculiar to the *Pygmies*. It was a common practice for the various ethnic groups of Africa which needed to trade in order to survive. This was an essential basis for the pre-colonial cooperation among the various ethnic groups of Africa even as they occasionally struggled to control major trade routes.[21]

The old societies (state and so called "stateless"), sometimes referred to as "primitive societies", espoused common characteristics even in diversity. They showed a strong desire to master a sense of justice, which was based on their perception of what was right, from wrong (moral sense). They were clearly suspicious of arbitrary or tyrannical rule, and, therefore, designed mechanisms to check authoritarian rule or what could otherwise be regarded as regal tyranny. This was normally done through a council, and, in the absence of a council, a form of mystic society where everyone was seen as equal on the basis of the fundamental right to be heard or to survive. Age old rules or adages informed political action. Kings and leaders were generally seen as *primus inter pares*, and were generally patrons of secret societies.

Secret societies functioned with some moral prerogatives and performed legislative and judicial functions. They also performed community service. These societies were aware that disputes were inevitable, and they developed methods of dealing with them before they became overwhelming. There was a general apprehension of extensive belligerence or genocidal wars, as was demonstrated by the *Nuer*. The sense of mutual assured destruction necessitated methods of conflict management or resolution, for which the *Leopard-Skin Chiefs* were instrumental.

What the "primitive societies" did was to have a public policy that would be responsive to aggregate interests and needs. In their own "dark world", this was as democratic as their societies could get given the circumstances and environments of their time. Yet, they were mindful of the causes of political adversity. The problem was that each group confronted the problem in its own way with its own sense of pride and superiority within its perceptible frontier. It was up to the superseding post-colonial state with modernized institutions to improve on the inheritance and manage the latent problem of ethnic pride. In the crises-ridden countries of Africa, the post-colonial state has failed in this endeavor. It is fairly certain that the new concept of the state has not taken hold in the volatile and impoverished nations of Africa. Until the concept of democracy or enlightened rule is well understood, and settled, the concept of political stability is still precarious in most of Africa. The ruined political state of affairs brings with it unimaginably woeful economic and social consequences that would continue for many years to come without deliberate efforts to fix political and economic problems.

Focus Questions

1. How did the pre-colonial societies check the authority of their rulers?
2. What role did traditional religion play as a moral force in the formation of pre-colonial societies?
3. What mechanisms were used by traditional societies to manage conflict and avert internecine wars?
4. To what extent would you argue that the traditional societies understood the need for co-operation and interdependence?

CHAPTER 2

BUILDING THE NEW AFRICAN STATES

The construction of the contemporary African states really started prior to the Berlin Conference of 1884/5. The Berlin Conference barely formalized the ongoing process of colonization and sought ways to legitimize new claims on Africa to avoid major European conflicts over the continent.

Conflicts were sure to emerge if spheres of influence were not well delineated. This meant carving up well-defined spheres of influence or boundaries. For one thing, the interest in Africa was growing as the Germans prepared for an aggressive colonial policy in Africa. In 1884, after negotiations with Great Britain, the Germans proclaimed a protectorate over Southwest Africa and eventually annexed what became known as German Cameroon.

In 1884, the German chancellor Otto von Bismarck called together the major western powers of the world to negotiate questions and preempt confusion over the control of Africa. The fourteen countries represented at the time were Austria-Hungary, Belgium, Denmark, France, Germany, Great Britain, Italy, the Netherlands, Portugal, Russia, Spain, Sweden-Norway (unified from 1814-1905), Turkey, and the United States of America. Of these nations, France, Germany, Great Britain, and Portugal controlled most of colonial Africa at the time and played a more active or dominant role in the conference.

An equally urgent task of the conference was to guarantee the neutrality of the mouths and basins of major rivers like the Congo and Niger. This was essential for trade although part of the Congo Basin became a personal property of Belgium's King Leopold II who unleashed unspectacular brutality over its inhabitants.

The bid for new acquisitions and legitimization of such acquisitions motivated the Europeans to control the hitherto uncontrolled interior of the continent. At the time of the conference, active colonization was mainly restricted to the coastal areas of Africa.[22] However, as the powers haggled and struggled for control over the continent, they oversighted or disregarded what were clearly the cultural variations and complexities of the continent.

The Berlin Conference was really a symptom of a looming problem, the problem of micromanaging the various societies which were to be found in the interior of the new European acquisitions. For example, this meant dealing with the *Nuers, Temnes, Mendes, Igbos, Limbas, Pygmies, Yorubas, Hutsis,* and *Tutsis*, and not just an educated or western-oriented class. The situation was even messier because the new set up meant making sure that the *Hutsis* could relate to the *Tutsis*, and the *Limba*s to the *Mendes* within the requirements of the new environment known as the "modern state". How could these diverse societies be ruled as one entity in the form of a western state? How could they coexist with the new demands on them?

The British Paradigm

To deal with the newly acquired conundrum, the British adopted a system of indirect rule. The system was predicated on the belief that the Africans and the Europeans were not necessarily unequal but distinct in terms of culture. The recognition of cultural differences meant the preservation of the traditional forms of government in the best way possible.

For obvious reasons, it was impossible to preserve the pre-colonial systems in their pristine form. First, there was the need for a liaison officer between the indigenous people and the British, who must be sympathetic to British interest. Second, the political structure of the natives must be conformable to the ambitions of colonialism. For example, chiefs must guarantee stability and must be willing and able to function as tax collectors for the new administration.

Indirect rule graduated from a much more aggressive and direct policy under Lord Lugard to a less aggressive and indirect policy after Lugard. Not all societies were easily understood by colonial administrators, and they were not easily amenable to the wishes of the colonial administration. For example, it was very problematic applying the idea of indirect rule to the *Igbos* and other southeastern tribes of Nigeria. Indirect rule meant the declaration of a protectorate over the natives of the interior. This meant that the natives of the interior became British protected subjects.

In theory, the areas that were considered protectorate were not liable to British jurisdiction. For example, Sir James Hay, who became Governor of Sierra Leone from 1881 to 1891 told a group of chiefs prior to the declaration of the protectorate that the Frontier Police, a paramilitary force established by Ordinance of the Legislative Council of Sierra Leone in January 1890, was forbidden to interfere with the rule of the chiefs. They were not expected to hold courts or exercise authority over the people they were stationed among. "Officers might settle small disputes if appealed to, but had to refer important decisions to the Governor, through the Department of Native Affairs."[23] Not even traders who failed to collect their debts were assured the assistance of the Frontier Police. The natives of Sierra Leone were officially granted protection in 1896.

Adjoining the protectorate was the colony which was established as the Crown Colony of 1808. Colonies were, for the most part, areas adjoining the sea with major maritime and port facilities. They were normally acquired by cession, annexation, or treaty. The colony of Sierra Leone was a fortuitous acquisition for the British because of the preponderance of *Creoles*, the inhabitants of the colony, who were well disposed to the adoption and spread of the British way of life. This gave them an aura of supremacy over the indigenes, who were seen as less exposed, primitive, barbaric, "uncivilized," and occasionally contemptuously referred to as "unto whom."

The word "*Creole/Krio*," suggests a status of crystallization and acquisition of political power that resulted from a mixture of Africans who were recaptured on the high seas (Recaptives) and resettled in the colony (which was known as Freetown), and upper class settler groups, predominantly Nova Scotians.[24] The Nova Scotians, largely of African and Maroon descent, were once in America where they spoke English, fought alongside the British during the American War of Independence, and acquired various skills as carpenters, masons, and shoe makers. They were eventually settled in the Nova Scotian province of Canada before repatriation to Freetown.[25] They had further embraced Christian values and had a workable knowledge of the English language. The stage was already set for many nations within a nation. What actually set the stage for subsequent ruin were not only the pattern of colonial administration and the conflicts that ensued out of that pattern, but also the manner in which the colonial administration dealt with the conflicts before departure.

The exit was vindictive for reasons that were both unfortunate and misguided. Simply put, the *Creoles* were responsible for the Hut Tax insurrection, which became known as "Cardew's War" of 1898—a treachery beyond comprehension. This paved the way for a recklessly overextended franchise, the hurried unification of colony and protectorate, and for less experience, mediocre, and corrupt politicians and/or bureaucrats to gain political power and perpetuate a reign of terror. Although the protectorate and the colony had been governed as two entities with discernibly different applications of laws, new reasons were forged for unification without proper experimentation or education. Why is it that the colonial administration never governed the two regions coherently until the moment of departure?

The underlying philosophy of British colonial administration was clear, *separate but equal*. As humans, the indigenes were not any different from the British or their *Creole* counterparts. They were clearly different on cultural matters, which certainly included notions of politics and religion.

The superimposition of western political beliefs created great cause for concern at the very outset of colonial rule for understandable reasons. First, its acceptability was not guaranteed. Second, understanding its operation and essence was an expensive proposition that required changing the lifestyle of people—a revolutionary undertaking. By 1895 the *laissez-faire-like* attitude to indigenous politics was changing.

The Foreign Jurisdiction Act of 1890 empowered the Crown to exercise jurisdiction claimed in a foreign country as if by right of conquest or cession. An Order-in-Council of August 28, 1895, empowered the Crown to acquire jurisdiction in foreign countries adjoining the colony, and, in 1892, Christopher Parkes, who became secretary to the Department of Native Affairs, drew up a plan for administering the interior.

One of the recommendations of Parkes was to have *Creoles* as agents for the administration of the interior with limited judicial powers, but London turned down the plan because the *Creoles* could not be trusted and London was less optimistic about finding five suitable ones. This was a lost opportunity for qualified Africans to take more responsibility for their government or advise the British on sensitive matters including taxes.

In 1898, the Hut Tax War broke out with far reaching political implications for trust, consensus, or harmony. Governor Frederick Cardew, who was responsible for the imposition of the tax, was clearly knowledgeable about fiscal policy but largely ignorant of traditional African beliefs. His ignorance was further clouded by his experience elsewhere, which replaced the danger of compositional fallacy, a generalized error in reasoning.

Adding the protectorate to areas already under British jurisdiction meant financial hardship. How was the administration of the protectorate to be paid for? This is not quite a puzzle for one with a western twist of mind. When a government is broke it could simply increase taxes, sell securities, or loan money. Alternatively, it could reduce spending, which paradoxically does not happen with increased government responsibility. The African environment, nevertheless, was an entirely different one. To the indigenes, taxes had implications beyond their evident fiscal connotation.

Cardew felt he could raise direct taxes in the protectorate. Why not? Taxes have been paid without difficulty in Zululand, Gambia, French Sudan and Liberia.[26] Therefore, they must be paid with no difficulty in the protectorate of Sierra Leone. He provided for an annual tax of ten shillings on houses in the protectorate with four rooms and five shillings on houses with fewer rooms, effective January 1, 1898. The Chiefs were to be responsible for collecting the house-tax with the aid of the District Commissioner, his Court Messengers, and if need be, the Frontier Police.

The tax was met with violent resistance, which resulted in the infamous "Hut Tax War." Foray chronicles four phases of the war: (i) operations in *Karene* and *Masimera* districts which were aimed at defeating the *Temne* chief, Bai Bureh and his allies; (ii) operations in Ronietta district; (iii) operations in Bandajuma and *Sherbro* districts; and (iv) the march through the protectorate in four columns between December 1898 and February 1899.

The tax was repugnant for a number of reasons. The indigenes mistook it for a loss of possession of their houses. The chiefs and their people further became suspicious of the new laws and regulations, which implied a loss of traditional authority. The problem with the war was not so much that it was fought to maintain independence and possession, but that it engendered damage, which is yet to be repaired among those who were supposed to coexist after colonialism.

The appreciable level of interaction that existed between the indigenes and the *Creoles* was severely jeopardized. Prior to the war, the *Creoles* ventured into the protectorate as traders, missionaries, and educators. As traders and missionaries, they brought hope and became agents of cultural diffusion. A significant amount of this foreign culture was later to be adopted in the process of integration into the global economy. These included Christianity, western education, western style of dressing, and an international language (English).

The process of acculturization was not peculiar to the protectorate. In the colony, children of indigenes were adopted and raised in the western tradition by *Creoles*. This experience was normally reflected in the names of the recipients of western exposure—normally a mixture of what is traditional and what is western. Examples included Alusine Kamara-Taylor (where Kamara is indigenous, and Taylor is western), and Foday Thomas (where Foday is indigenous, and Thomas is western).

During the Hut Tax War, thousands of *Creoles* who had formed the bridge between the colonial administration and the indigenes were hacked to death. Murdered bodies of *Creoles* were burnt or thrown into sea. The revolt had wider ramifications than the hatred of the tax. It was indiscriminately against everything western. The *Creoles* suddenly became the stooges of the colonial administration and a more accessible outlet for vengeance. They were blamed for everything western including the house-tax. The colonial administration, on the other hand, blamed the *Creoles* for inciting the rebellion. In actual fact, the position of the *Creoles* on the tax was unambiguous.

The *Creoles* opposed the tax at its inception and made their opinions known in various newspapers in Freetown. Men and women alike opposed the tax. Fyfe writes:

> Women gathered outside Government House and held
> A prayer-meeting, processing round the garden wall,
> singing hymns, praying that a miracle soften the Governor's
> hard heart.[27]

If not for anything, the mutual dislike of some prominent *Creoles* for the Governor, and the Governor for such *Creoles* made it impossible for the Governor to relent or revisit his position on the tax issue. The obdurate Governor who had just been knighted in 1897 was less passionate about the administration of the protectorate.

> Neuralgia, shingles, insomnia, racked his powerful frame,

> Exaggerating his irritability, making him suspicious of advice quick to offence and impute evil motives. Distaste for the law cut him off from the senior officials, his natural associates, as firmly as from Lewis, and confirmed his inclination to rule alone.[28]

The grievances of the chiefs were real and specific. Colonial administration had not functioned as it was intended. The Frontier Police was uncontrollable and, in many places of the interior, its members assumed despotic powers terrorizing the chiefs and people, seized their goods, and brutalized those who protested. It was not uncommon for the wife of the member of the force to be imposed as a chief. Could there be calm after the storm?

The episodes that ultimately led to the constitutional changes and the creation of post-colonial state were rancorous and full of deep-seated animosities. In the already volatile situation, what form of government should be established? What political philosophy? One country, one nation? Separate but equal? Who had the experience to nurture the burgeoning form of the western democratic state to ensure its preservation? Was the country properly prepared for the task at hand? Was it accustomed to the new form of government it was about to take on?

Kup dates the beginning of modern politics in Sierra Leone at 1909.[29] This was the year when the Rate Payers Association was formed with the important objective of contesting elections to the Municipal Council. In rapid and successive order, there was soon a mushroom of political organizations, which sought an outlet for representation and audience. The protectorate's first political organization was the Committee of Educated Aborigines, which was formed in the 1920s to voice the interests of the educated elites in the protectorate, but it had, as a larger objective, the representation of the interests of the protectorate. It eventually became the protectorate Educational Progressive Union (PEPU).

The major catapult to constitutional change during the 1920s was the National Congress of British West Africa (NCBWA). The organization was founded in 1920, with branches in Gambia, Sierra Leone, and Nigeria. Its members were mostly drawn from the educated and professional/business classes, which pointedly criticized colonial rule. The demands of the organization were normally couched in resolutions, which were sent to the Secretary of State for the colonies in the form of petitions.

The early demands of the organization did not call for immediate independence, but they made modest requests for more African representation in the Legislative Councils, the provision of Municipal Councils and Houses of Assembly, and reforms in education, part of which was the provision of a West African University. Although the Governors tried as best as possible to foil or thwart the ambitions of the organizations, oftentimes referring to them in disparaging manner as pretentious, ill-intentioned, and not representative of native wishes, the organization realized marginal successes. African representation increased marginally.

The latent problems soon emerged. Who will represent the unenlightened? Who should legislate for whom? The enlightened portion had assumed that they were destined to secure the interest of the unenlightened. "The enlightened portion of West Africa is responsible for the unenlightened portion... It is a right justified by the kinship of Race and Blood".[30] The political squabbles over the first constitutional concession of 1924 were immediate and poignant. The 1924 constitution, known as the Slater Constitution, after the Governor Sir Alexander Slater, made provision for the first elected unofficials of the Legislative Council. The last time there had been any form of constitutional amendment was in 1863 under Governor Samuel Blackall. It was then that the Governor's Council, which had served as an all-purpose body, was broken up into Executive and Legislative Councils.[31] What made the 1924 constitution so contentious?

The constitution made provision for ten unofficial members of the Legislative Council: (i) two were to represent commercial and general European interests; (ii) three elected members represented Freetown, *Sherbro*, and the Rural Areas; (iii) two were to be nominated from the colony; and (iv) three from the protectorate. The *Creoles* objected to protectorate representation in the Legislative Council under the 1890 Foreign Jurisdiction Act, which made it illegal for British protected peoples and aliens to legislate for British subjects. This was one of several issues which were not resolved satisfactorily by independence in 1961.

The political dichotomy between colony and protectorate was taken seriously by some *Creole* elements in the colony, especially the likes of Dr. Bankole-Bright who were calling for a secession of the colony from the protectorate. In fact, the manifesto of his political party, the National Council of the Colony of Sierra Leone (NCCSL), clearly opposed "foreigners prepondering" in the Legislative Council. In graphic terms he saw the protectorate and colony as two mountains separated by a deep and wide valley that would never meet.

Although the colonial administration had been suspected of grass root political participation and limited the degree of political participation to the educated and tax payers, by the 1940s, there was an extraordinary effort to adopt universal adult suffrage, which never really materialized until the moment of independence.

The new Governor, Sir Beresford-Stooke, who arrived in Freetown to succeed Governor Stevenson, was particularly sympathetic to the cause of the educated elites of the protectorate. He advocated for a careful balance between an expression of the opinion of the common people and the educated classes in particular. Until the late 1950s and prior to independence, the colony qualifications for voting as determined by the Keith Lucas Commission (1957) had been based on £60.0 (sixty pounds) per annum or residence of a property with value of £2.0 (two pounds). In the protectorate, there had never been any franchise to vote. Adult men and women (21 years and older) liable to pay taxes could now vote.

The *Creoles* seldom did anything to make the colonial administration comfortable. Lewis, Dr. Bankole-Bright, Beoku-Betts, and Akuna Wallace-Johnson were hardly politically correct. It was fairly apparent that their "harmful" demagoguery and opposition to taxes, or sympathy with the "toiling masses" were a constant source of embarrassment to Governors and colonial administrators alike. Their obsession with rights and sympathy for workers made them more of saboteurs than collaborators in the eyes of the colonial administration, and by the time of independence in 1961, there was virtually nothing for which the *Creoles* could have been rewarded by the colonial administration. All was not well.

The political parties that came into existence struggled to take on a national dimension or appeal, but espoused affectionate ethnic or regional proclivities. The Sierra Leone's People Party (SLPP), founded in 1951, had presumed by its motto, "one country one people," that Sierra Leone is "one country" with/for "one people." This was an obvious challenge to what Foray calls "*Creole* dominance and *Creole* pretensions."[32] The SLPP was, in reality, a Southern-based political party although it had a somewhat diverse membership.

There was also the All People's Congress (APC), which was first launched as a call for Elections Before Independence Movement (EBIM) in July of 1960. The leaders were predominantly northerners and it originally unambiguously identified itself with the north. The movement was an attempt to challenge the national legitimacy of the United Front Coalition (UFC), the government that was to lead the country into independence. Squabbles existed over national defense and finance, and the lack of expertise among Sierra Leoneans negotiating independence with the colonial office. The submissive posture of the leaders of the SLPP was in Siaka Steven's opinion, "independence with strings".[33]

Some other political parties included the NCCSL/NC which was founded as a virtually *Creole* party in 1950, the Sierra Leone Independence movement (SLIM) in 1956, and the Sierra Leone Progressive Independence movement (SLPIM) in 1959. By 1962, SLPIM included the Kono Progressive Movement (KPM), which was formed in 1955 with the express purpose of protesting agreements between the Sierra Leone Government and the Sierra Leone Selection Trust (SLST), a diamond mining company. Members wanted the use of the resource primarily for the *Konos*.

At the end of colonial rule, it was apparent that if there was to be any form of stability, the post colonial state needed not only prudent, enlightened and disciplined rulers, but a political climate which was essential to nurture and preserve the concept of a modern democratic state.

The problems associated with British colonialism in Sierra Leone were not radically different from that in the Sudan. As in Sierra Leone, there were calls for territorial secession prior to independence on the grounds that the North and the South were administered as two separate regions by the British, and that the two regions were culturally different. The North is made up of predominantly Arab-Africans who are Muslims, and the South, is mostly populated by Christian or animist Africans. A dual political system goes back to the 1820s after the Egyptian conquest of the Sudan. The Egyptians claimed the entire territory, but were never really able to extend control over the South, which remained fragmented along tribal lines and attracted marauding slave raiding attacks.

After the British gained control of the Sudan in the 1930s, the Sudan was divided into regions and ruled as such with some amount of sensitivity to the ethnic and religious differences. Northern Islamic influence was largely confined to the North and largely excluded from the South. As the demands for independence became louder, particularly from Northerners in Khartoum for self-rule, there was tremendous pressure on the British to maintain the country as one composite.

The Egyptians exerted pressure on the British to unify the North and the South with the hope that the country might have been part of Egypt. For one thing, the Egyptians and the British had worked together and maintained a condominium over the Sudan in the late 1890s after the suppression of the *Mahdist* Revolution in 1898. Exclusion of the North from the South also meant exclusion from economic projects in the South—an economic alienation.

In 1953, Egypt, the Northerners, and the British signed an agreement for self-determination. The opinions of the Southerners were largely marginalized and discounted, and boundary delineations were made with utter disregard for social or ethnic realities. The fundamental problem with boundary settlements prior to decolonization was that they made it extremely difficult, if not impossible, to conjure up any sense of realistic national aspirations. The situation was made worse when no official policy was developed, as in Singapore, to deal with the problem of ethnic tensions. The situation was ripe for rebellion.

The South became mutinous and several Northerners were killed. In the state of flux and confusion, Sudan was granted independence in 1956 to tend to its affairs. The situation in Sudan was interesting for a number of reasons. For example, unlike the cosmetic show of nationalism in British West Africa, there was never a clear or ostensible show of nationalism in Sudan, which made the post-colonial reconstruction even more difficult. For intermittent and protracted periods, there has been civil strife in the South, and civil wars in the Sudan.

The failed state is the result of the lack of adequate safety net in the post-colonial reconstruction of the Sudan. Independence was hoped to have been achieved under a system of federalism that would accommodate ethnic and social differences. The compromise never took place, but it rather was replaced by a system of Islamization and/or Arabization—a transformation or corruption of the British policy of indirect rule to that of assimilation used by the French in the formative years of French colonial policy.

The French Paradigm

In 1659, the French established a trade port at St. Louis (present day Senegal), on the west coast of Africa, but they never participated actively in the rush for African territories until later in the nineteenth century. The efforts of the French were mostly focused on the Senegal River area and its hinterland, an area from which the French implemented their prototype policy of assimilation.

Jules Ferry, who was twice appointed Prime Minister of France between 1880 and 1885, was largely responsible for the French colonial expansion in the nineteenth century. His speech before the French Chamber of Deputies, March 28, 1884, laid the basis for three fundamental principles of French colonial policy: (i) the economic necessity of acquiring colonies; (ii) the necessity for the "higher races" to civilize the "lower races;" and (iii) a patriotic duty.[34]

The case made by Ferry was intended to draw attention to the fact that America was thoroughly protectionist and that Germany, one of France's neighbors was actively setting up barriers to trade. There was a compelling and urgent need for outlets to export French goods. The economic and social conditions of Ferry's time needed a great patriotic awakening, one that would support his plans for colonization.

Early French colonial policy meant two things: (i) subjugation or conquest of the "heathen" peoples of Africa; and (ii) civilization, the ultimate goal of assimilation. After General Louis Faidherbe was appointed Governor of Senegal in 1854, the French began a major movement eastward into the savanna regions of Africa.

The Governor-General in Dakar was to report to, and to take his orders from the Minister of Colonies and the government in Paris. In the interior of French West Africa, the territories were headed by Lieutenant-Governors who worked as subordinates of a Governor-General.

Assimilation formed part of French political administration in Senegal. Africans could represent four municipalities, otherwise known as communes (Dakar, Gorée, Rufisque and St. Louis), in France. Whilst the British were improvising a system of political administration, the French were implementing a system they were already familiar with, the communes. Assimilation was an essential process to acquiring citizenship, which conferred the political privilege of voting Deputies to the French Assembly/parliament. The acquisition of French citizenship was evidently based on the renunciation of "primitive" African culture. Education and income became indicators of status crystallization in the process of transition. The French colonies basically became appendages to France. This system was destined to work fairly well for as long as the possession of France was not very extensive.

Once France's possession of colonies became fairly extensive, the system of assimilation as an administrative method became clumsy. For example, rather than adhering to the proto-type system of direct administration, Tunisia and Morocco were declared protectorates. This system was not radically different from the British system of indirect rule and the reasons for its adoption were not significantly different from what the British had experienced. There were two basic common denominators: (i) the cost of administering large territories and (ii) accommodating the indigenous culture to prevent widespread and pervasive rebellion.

Assimilation proved to be an expensive proposition. Apart from the general renunciation of "primitive" culture, which was very demanding, the clash of Christian and Islamic values proved to be an enduring and fierce conflict. Devout Muslims saw the French as adversaries and infidels, and, by 1848, France had already resigned itself to the idea that Islam and Islamic courts could not be eradicated. The first of the Islamic courts in the four communes was opened in St. Louis in 1848, and Africans who became French citizens could still be subjected to the jurisdiction of Islamic courts.

Many of the African states were once independent societies that relished their independence and autonomy in relation to other African groups. When they became apprehensive of domination by local neighbors, they signed treaties of friendship with European powers for protection, but, by so doing, they were not willing to give up their independence. For example, Sikasso signed a treaty of friendship with the French for protection against Samory (another local leader). However, when the French wanted to assert rights, which were *ultra-vires* the rights of protection, Sikasso teamed up with Samory to fight the French.[35] There was something that was plausibly intuitive about the dealings of Africans with the Europeans during the formative years of European expansion in Africa. The local African leaders seemed to have dealt with the Europeans with the hope of protecting their autonomy rather than losing it to their local neighbors or the Europeans. Local autonomy was something that was jealously guarded before colonial rule and it was never significantly restored after colonial rule in crisis-ridden African countries. The neglect of local autonomy in the post-colonial state has fostered exploitation and widespread allocative or distributive problems in countries that have failed to adopt a carefully balanced decentralized approach to government.

French colonialism was also extended to Central Africa. The French colonies of Gabon, Congo (Brazzaville), and Ubanghi-Chari or Ubangi-Shari (Central African Republic) were collectively referred to as French Equatorial Africa (AEF). Each territory was placed under a French officer known as a commandant. The commandant presided over canton chiefs (chiefs of political subdivisions/cantons). The commandant was under no obligation to respect the traditional African principles of government. The colonial administration instituted by the French was intent on preventing any coalescence of opposition that would threaten the existence of French rule.

In the pre-colonial period, three kingdoms dominated the republic of the Congo: Kongo, the *Loango*, and *Tio*. After the Portuguese located the Congo River in 1482, contacts were made with the tribes, and that opened the way for subsequent contacts.

In 1880, Pierre Savorgnan de Brazza signed a treaty on behalf of the French with *Makoko*, a ruler of the *Bateke* people. Thereafter, French rule was established in what was first called French Congo. In the Congo as well as West Africa, the French were rather harsh in their administrative attempts to increase their political control and economic gains over their colonies. Familiar methods included "divide and rule", forced labor (*courvee*) and the application of the *indigénant*, a code of law which was applied and arbitrarily enforced since 1887.

Abuse of laborers aroused public outcry and rebellions among the Congolese. Magbaily-Fyle observes that forced labor in the AEF was more rampant and controlled by the colonial administration. "People forcefully drafted to work were not even provided with food. They had to be fed by the local community within walking distance of their place of work."[36] It was not uncommon for forced labor to be used in the construction of infrastructure, which resulted in massive fatalities. It is reported that the Fang population was reduced from 140,000 to 65,000 during the construction of a railway from Congo to Océan by 1933.[37] Colonialism, in its political form, was destined to die.

Some British espoused a desire to end colonialism in the 1850s even before the French made a feverish rush to acquire colonies in the 1880s. Gladstone, who was Chancellor of the Exchequer in Lord Aberdeen's Government of 1852-5, was critical of the duration of colonialism then. He found an unlikely ally in Disraeli, who also served as Chancellor of the Exchequer for a very brief period in 1852. Their agreement on the dissolution of the British colonial empire was best summarized by Disraeli, who made a portentous 1852 declaration: "These wretched colonies will all be independent in a few years and are millstones around our necks."[38]

The British as well as the French faced a formidable opposition to colonial rule, and the World Wars sapped their strength and resolution, or even the possibility of maintaining large colonial empires. In the AEF tensions were already on the ascendancy by the 1930s, the nature of which exemplified revulsion at colonial rule. Yet, at the heart of the dissension, even as the Africans were in a hurry to get rid of the yoke of colonial rule, there was very little indication that there was a readily available viable alternative system of government to supplant the French colonial administration. This was not an uncommon dilemma for former colonial territories that wrestled with the problem of reconciling parochial local interests or autonomy (which existed before colonialism) with that of the national interests (which came after the post-colonial state). For example, it would be recalled that a similar problem existed in Sierra Leone.

In August 1940, General DeGaulle called on the AEF to fight for a free France. After the war, the French Constitution of 1946 was inaugurated as the first of a series of reforms which were to lead eventually to self rule for all the French territories in West and Equatorial Africa. Africans were further encouraged to execute a concerted opposition to colonial rule in the 1940s.

Bartélemy Boganda formed the pro-independence Social Evolution Movement of Black Africa, *Mouvement d'Evolution Sociale de l'Afrique Noire* (MESAN), in 1941, and demanded basic rights. This movement targeted the dissolution of French colonial rule and preached a message of social change and liberty. It was not unlike the other independence movements in its aim to end colonial rule.

The French and British approach to decolonization and the granting of rights had some remarkable similarities. Although the British did not grant widespread citizenship to the indigenous people, who until the verge of independence were considered protected subjects, the British afforded them voting privileges which had hitherto been denied prior to independence. The 1946 constitution made provisions for French citizenship to be extended to all inhabitants, and establishment of local assemblies.

The preamble to the October 1946 constitution reaffirmed the "inalienable and sacred rights" of man regardless of race, religion or creed, which had been upheld by the 1789 Declaration of the Rights of Man. It also indicated France's intention to allow the Africans to be somewhat responsible for their own democratic governments. The idea of colonialism by the arbitrary use of power was unequivocally rejected and a promise was made to guarantee everyone access to public office.

The desire to relinquish total control over the colonial territories and to provide for elective office was enacted in Article 79 of the 1946 constitution. Overseas territories were to elect representatives of the national Assembly and Council of the Republic within the conditions laid down by the law. The French inclination to provide elective office was complemented by the granting of citizenship in the same way that nationals of Metropolitan France could acquire citizenship. Article 82 guaranteed equal protection to those who did not desire French citizenship. In 1946, Bartélemy Boganda, the founder of MESAN, became the first African to be elected to the French parliament. Ten years later, the *Basic Law* of June 23, 1956, eliminated voting inequalities and provided opportunities for the branches of government that were essential for the independence of the individual territories.

The constitutional referendum of September 1958, led to dissolution of AEF and further expansion of the internal powers of the former overseas territories, which became known as autonomous republics. The Central African Republic (Ubanghi-Chari/Ubangi-Shari) officially became autonomous on December 1, 1958, and an independent nation on August 13, 1960.

With rare exceptions, it did not take long for the new élites to show their incompetence or to dissociate themselves from the ideals of liberty and freedom that they were so passionate about prior to independence. In the elections of 1957, MESAN had an impressive success. It captured all the assembly seats and obtained all the posts in the new cabinet. In 1958, Boganda the priest turned politician became the first prime minister of Central African Republic, but his government enacted electoral laws that were designed to perpetuate MESAN control of political power. Opposition parties were disqualified prior to the 1959 elections.

The Belgian Paradigm

There is widespread agreement among historians that Leopold II of Belgium espoused the most egregious atrocities in the conduct of colonial policy. Belgium ruled the Congo and inherited the colonies of Rwanda and Burundi from

Germany after Germany lost the First World War and her colonies in Africa. However, interestingly, the Belgian Congo (Zaire/Congo Democratic Republic) was the only country in Africa that was ruled as the personal property of a foreign sovereign from 1878 to 1908. During the period of individual ownership, the Congo was generally referred to as the Congo Free State until it was transferred over to the Belgian government in 1908.

The ambitions of Leopold I to expand the commercial prospects of Belgium were seized in avid terms by his successor. The convocation of the international geographic conference at Brussels on September 12, 1876, at his request was largely intended to end the demoded trade in slaves as well as to "civilize" backward Africans. The convocation, which seems to have been a fruitful meeting of Germany, Austria-Hungary, France, Great Britain, Italy, Russia and Belgium, facilitated the formation of a new organization, the International African Association. The aims of the association were to be achieved through exploratory expeditions, and the establishment of hospitals and scientific posts.

Leopold II

True to the ideals of the International African Association, aggressive plans of exploration and discovery were pursued. By 1878, Stanley made a successful expedition down the Congo River. This was not the most promising of prospects for Leopold II, but the lukewarm reception that was given to Stanley by Britain and America turned out to be very fortuitous for Leopold's personal ambitions. Stanley teamed up with Leopold II.

In November of 1878, a committee for the study of the Upper Congo was set up in collaboration with businessmen. This committee was, however, supplanted by the International Association of the Congo. Various commercial activities took place in the Congo and communication lines were opened up. The accomplishment of Leopold II somewhat neutralized the envy and potential rivalry among the Great powers. Out of this precarious and fragile situation, Leopold was able to carve for himself a state in Africa, which gained some amount of recognition by the Berlin Conference of 1884/5. In April 1885, the Belgian Parliament authorized Leopold II to be the head of the new state founded in Africa. The new stipulation of the parliament also made it possible for the relationship between Belgium and the new state to rest on the prerogative of the sovereign. The basis of ruthless imperialism was laid. On July 19, 1885 a proclamation of the accession to the throne of the Congo Free State by Leopold II was made with widespread publicity to all powers. In as much as Berlin gave tacit approval to Leopold II, Leopold's possession of the Congo was contingent on actual and effective occupation of the country. He, therefore, mustered all the assistance he could get to legitimize his claim on the Congo. Much was desired and needed.

One of the earliest challenges that confronted Leopold II was the construction of a railroad, which was to link *Matadi* and *Leopoldville*. The railway would enable him to foster rubber production and improve commerce by connecting the navigable sections of the Lower Congo and the Upper Congo. The rail construction also required tremendous labor, which had to be imported when local supply proved to be inadequate.

The Belgian strategy was to rule the Congo through concession companies, often times giving those companies exclusive rights, and to acquire labor by force. Forced labor was essential to mine precious minerals and cultivate land at abysmally low costs. The initial concern of cultivation was focused on rubber to supply European industry. As Fyle puts it, "[i]n both the Congo and neighboring Angola, rubber became the king in the 1890s and 1900s. Rubber exports from the Congo rose from two tons in 1891 to 6,000 tons in 1901."[39] The rubber exploits of the Congo caused excessive hardship to the local population, which was coerced into submission and made to toil under inexorable directions of company officials and their ad hoc armies. Fyle records part of the atrocities as follows:

> Quotas were given to villages, which if not fulfilled, meant the destruction of villages, shooting of inhabitants and frequent cutting off of limbs, breasts and ears of the people. One European visitor reported a supervisor counting the number of hacked limbs to ensure that bullets supplied had not been wasted.[40]

Large numbers of men were worked to death, as Leopold's ad hoc army raped and starved their wives to make them work harder to collect wild rubber. The net effect of colonial rule in the Congo terrified hundreds of thousands of people who fled to other neighboring countries to avoid the rubber slavery. The harsh and appalling labor conditions under Leopold II reduced the population of the Congo by about 73 percent.

In 1908, the Belgian government took over the Congo, but not entirely at the largesse of Leopold II, who in 1889 had willed that the Congo and all sovereign rights be transmitted to Belgium after his death. The Belgian government obviously had a stake in the colonization of the Congo after it loaned Leopold II 25 million Francs in 1890. The government had to be guaranteed that the loan would be repaid. This guarantee came with the option to annex the Congo after ten years. It also provided opportunities for the debt to be paid through the integration of the Congo with Belgium. As a matter of fact, Leopold II tried to stave off the annexation of the Congo until a later date when he believed the Congo would be much more productive. The Belgian government begged to differ. On August 20, 1908, the Belgian government passed a law, which paved the way for the annexation of the Congo.

Congo Democratic Republic (CDR/Zaire)

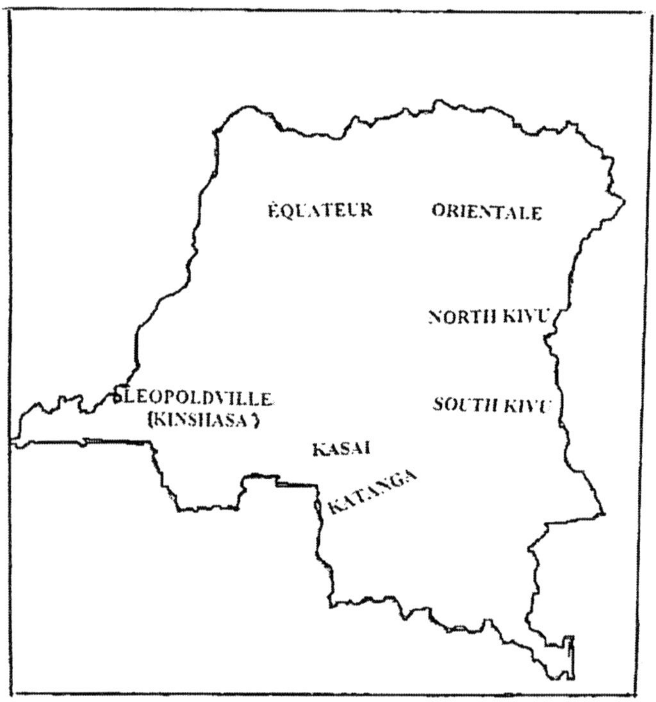

The Belgian control of the Congo provided comparatively much more humane conditions as prior atrocities fizzled. Inhumane conditions paled in comparison to what had hitherto existed under the Congo Free State. While the Belgians built schools, hospitals, roads and bridges, and siphoned profits to nations abroad, very little was done to prepare the Congolese for independence. The Congolese had scanty opportunity to witness or practice democracy and were generally clueless about the free market system. Independence came abruptly after several protests culminating in those of the 1960s. It is doubtful whether the Congolese had any serious thought as to how they could rule themselves except to get rid of their oppressors and constitute a replacement government.

The reforms that paved the way for a modern system of government in the Congo really started in 1910 after the death of Leopold II in December 1909. The Belgian Secretary of the Colonies, Jules Renkin, and the new King, Albert I, started some meaningful reforms to remove restrictions from trade and to modernize the tax system. Taxation in kind was abolished by decree and the money economy replaced the backward barter system. For once the native chieftains were brought in to take part in the new British-styled indirect rule in the Congo.

Belgium largely governed the Congo by decrees, and the Colonial Charter of October 1908, which was alternatively regarded as special laws. The decrees were stipulations of the king in his capacity as a legislator. Although the decrees of the King were subordinated to Acts of Parliament, in reality, the King made laws for the colonies and did not delegate such an authority.

The Colonial Charter contained articles borrowed from the Belgian Constitution. Like the French Declaration of Rights, the Colonial Charter provided for various freedoms, some of which included the freedom of the individual, freedom of religion, freedom to have an opinion, freedom to seek employment, freedom to own property, and freedom from censorship. These fundamental rights, which constitute the entrenched clauses of constitutions in modern democratic societies, were provisions Africans were less acquainted with prior to independence. Customary laws were given some recognition in so far as they did not conflict with written law. On June 30, 1960, the Congo gained independence from Belgium.

Like the other pre-colonial crises-ridden countries of Africa, it was not long before post-colonial Zaire fell into morass. Two reasons with widespread ramifications are particularly prominent: (i) the inability of African leaders to share political power or be accountable and (ii) the failed boundary delineations of the 1884/5 Berlin Conference.

In the first post-colonial elections, two prominent nationalists won: Patrice Lumumba of the leftist and militant *Mouvement National Congolais* (MNC) became prime minister, and Joseph Kasavubu of the *L'Allinace des Bakongo* (ABAKO) party became head of state. The formation of the MNC goes back to 1959 with territorial nationalist aspirations. Its declared objective inveighed against colonialism and called for the "emancipation of the Congo." How nationalistic the party was is subject to debate. However, its radicalism and intolerance under Lumumba caused it to splinter into factions under the moderate and competing leadership of Cyrille Adoula, and Albert Kalonji. The factionalism was clearly intended to appeal to limited religious support or to salvage the diminished stature of the MNC. Zaire was already divided into six regions: (i) *Orientale*; (ii) *Équateur;* (iii) *Leopoldville*; (iv) *Kivu*; (v) *Kasai*; and (vi) *Katanga*. Cyrille Adoula and Albert Kalonji wanted to deprive Lumumba of support in *Kasai* and *Katanga*.

The two elections of May 1960 and June 1960 further complicated the political situation. In May 1960, Lumumba had the largest number of votes but not the majority. The victory was, however, sufficient for the Belgian authorities to recognize Lumumba as Prime Minister. The June 1960 election made the ABAKO leader, Joseph Kasavubu, President. The two leaders were philosophically diametrically opposed and nurtured different brands of nationalism. There was not even an agreed perception of what was to constitute the Congolese state. The state was ripe for a civil war.

Immediately after independence, the *Force Publique*, which was supposed to maintain peace and stability, mutinied because it was less Africanized. The mutiny resulted in lawlessness and provided fertile opportunity for the start of secessionist movements. On July 11, 1960, *Katanga*, the richest mining province seceded from the union declaring its independence under Moise Tshombe. Shortly thereafter, the *Kasai* (*Kasai-Oriental* region) province followed. The *Katangan* secession was comparable to the *Biafran* secession movement. It indicated in clear terms the failure of transition from colonialism to independence and the inability of the Congolese leaders to resolve their differences which were obviously fueled by the potential for economic gain, rein- forced by ethnic and regional differences.

The secession of *Katanga* was disastrous for several reasons. A considerable number of Belgians were killed in *Katanga*. The Belgian government sent paratroopers to stop the civil war and protect its citizens. To the extent that the Congolese were unprepared for civil government, the effective functioning of the bureaucracy was crippled as the Belgians left the country in mass numbers. The conflict between Kasavubu and Lumumba necessitated a United Nations peacekeeping force in an extraordinary situation when there was no peace to keep or sides to take. Lumumba was eventually assassinated in 1961 under controversial circumstances.

The *Katangan* and *Biafran* secessionist movements were symptomatic of the deep-seated ethnic animosities that accompanied some African countries into the twentieth and twenty-first centuries. Prominent examples of the problems showed up in Rwanda, the Sudan, and, to a lesser and largely unnoticeable extent, Freetown. These problems will be dealt with in the next chapter.

At the end of colonial rule, colonized African states were clearly left with the following challenges: (i) synthesizing the diverse ethnic interests, catering for them, or respecting them within the newly carved territories; (ii) constituting and maintaining accountable systems of government; (iii) promoting general and civic education essential for nation building and individual achievement; (iv) integrating the two-sector economy; (iv) reforming the demoded infrastructure; (v) competing in the global economy, which involves the attraction of foreign investment or capital to offset inadequate saving; and (vi) prudent fiscal and monetary policies to promote growth and reduce poverty. These challenges were largely sacrificed because of the desire to consolidate political power and to isolate less fortunate or opposing groups.

Salient aspects of the tortuous, formative, evolving, and somewhat discerning pre-colonial politics were disturbed and eventually ostracized. The obvious differences between the pre-colonial African political system and the modern, made the marriage of the two extremely difficult to mesh without the required commitment and skill. The foundations of turmoil were laid.

A significant number of African leaders and élites who claimed to be able to unify their newly carved countries and to rectify the problems of colonial rule proved to be callously inept to deal with the challenge of emancipating their peoples from bondage and oppression, and providing them a better life. Some contemporary African states in crises more often than not espouse policies that are evidently reminiscent of the colonial past, and often times, worse. Much is still to be desired of African rulers who manifest utter disregard for the life of their citizens. More shocking is the persistence of "divide and conquer" as a principle of despotic government which gained notoriety in the nineteenth century. The adoption of despotism as a substitute to accountability continues to fuel the conditions for alienation, instability and genocide.

The post-colonial governments have generally failed to integrate the rural sector into the urban, or to reconstitute the two-sector economy created by colonial administration. One of the clear vestiges of colonial rule was the creation of two worlds— urban and agrarian (where the rural/agrarian is generally faithful to customs and clans and the other is outgoing and modernized). The mentalities of the two worlds seldom converge in any meaningful way. It is not uncommon for inhabitants of the rural sector to be seen in condescending or derogatory terms, or for the inhabitants of the rural region to be suspect of modernization. Urban life and privileges often become covetous, and act as a center of gravity. The dual economy has posed serious challenges to the development of the African economy. Migration to cities from decrepit and infra-structurally backward rural areas continues to threaten the economic viability of these African economies. The visible effects are growing problems of urbanization, and decline in farm output, which put an upward pressure on the import of food. It is not uncommon for adverse politics to encourage rural-urban migration. For example, in Sierra Leone of the 1970s and 1980s, politicians soliciting votes in a pseudo-democratic process encouraged an influx of gun-toting men from the interior or rural areas to cast votes for them in urban constituencies and often times intimidated their challengers.

The political philosophy of the new élites—that opposition must be discouraged and that political power must be consolidated at the end of colonialism, ushered in a protracted period of political instability, carnage, civil wars, excessive loss of lives, long-lasting adverse economic policies, and underdevelopment. It is certainly not easy to explain the possessive culture of post-colonial administration, yet, two things are readily apparent: (i) a lack of adequate exposure to democratic government or institutions prior to independence, and (ii) the idiosyncratic or arrogant predisposition of political leaders to think that they own the state for their personal enrichment and glory.

The European political system that came close to this perception flourished in the eighteenth century when kings identified themselves with absolute rule and the ancient idea that they had a divine right to rule. This was the ancient regime that was ably exemplified by Louis XIV and the phrase, "I am the state" (*L'état c'est moi*). Most of the post-colonial African states showed no radical departure from this eighteenth century political philosophy for the greater part of the twentieth century.

Focus Questions

1. How did the colonial state change the political structure of the pre-colonial societies?
2. To what extent could the British, French and Belgian colonial policies be differentiated?
3. Did the delineation of artificial boundaries by the Berlin Congress (1884/5) establish the basis for political and economic havoc in African States?
4. To what extent were the Africans granted ownership of political administration before the eventual independence of their states?
5. Were the African élites rash and insincere in their presumption of nationalism and call for political independence? Why?
6. The secessionist movements in Africa were a symptom of failed colonial and post-colonial policies. Is this a plausible assertion? Why

CHAPTER 3

COLONIALISM OR POLICY?

Once the dust settled down after colonial rule, some African leaders perfected the art of constitutional maneuver to prolong their stay in power. Three things were accorded urgency: (i) constitutional amendments to insure some form of legitimacy (fraud); (ii) the creation of a one party state; and (iii) providing the instruments of coercion needed to repel challengers or opponents. These were political calculations or decisions with adverse economic implications. The net effect of these policies was to ensure that the rulers determine the direction of their states, which has proved to be disastrous.

L'état c'est moi

Historians are not generally certain whether Louis XIV uttered the phrase, *L'état c'est moi*, but his style of leadership exemplified such a notion. In a much more convoluted sense, it was a style akin to the so-called "Age of Absolutism". Not only are historians not sure whether he uttered the phrase, political scientists doubt whether his reign could best be classified as that of "absolutism" since absolutism never obtained finality (not even under Bodin or Hobbes). What might resemble an analogy here is not an atavism of such a conception, but in an analogous sense to show the extent to which the authority of some African leaders remain unchecked and how they use state power to obtain personal and limited objectives.

Between 1960 and the debt crises of the 1980s, some African leaders lost opportunities to lay the foundations for growth as they consolidated political power, siphoned money abroad and repressed their people. The Cold War was on ascendancy and with that, the nonaligned movement. Favorable opportunities for growth included much more diversified opportunities for aid, and comparatively favorable exchange rates or low levels of inflation. Exogenous factors that significantly attenuated the full prospects of growth were the oil crises and the accompanying increase in the level of indebtedness associated with the crisis for the poor countries. What was really endogenous were the deliberate and flawed policies adopted by some African leaders in the post-independent period.

The creation of the one-party state was clearly intended to zap or discourage opposition and all forms of healthy debates about alternative theories of growth or use of public funds. The larger and apparent repercussion is that elections are really meaningless in these one-party states and they facilitate a tremendous waste of limited resources. They make no meaningful provision for competing views that challenge the interests and aspirations of the established authority or party (which is not a dominant party). Elections are, therefore, a sham and less responsive to the needs or wishes of a broader category of citizens. Opposition to sitting authority easily becomes treasonable and opponents who dare to raise embarrassing questions of a sitting regime become good candidates for execution.

There are more serious consequences over time. In a world that lacks enough benevolent despots, a government that is not accountable to its citizens perpetuates bad policies with no prospect of rectification. The citizenry could neither correct the government when it is wrong, nor kick it out of office. A government, therefore, functions on its own accord by implementing ruinous policies that are at variance with the general aspirations or national interests of the citizenry. Such an approach sets the stage for political and economic decay. The oppressed find outlets to register their revulsion, and the stage is set for protracted confrontation and hostilities.

In most of the post-colonial African societies, outlets for protests are normally in the form of violent demonstrations, military *coups*, or civil wars. In reality, the political choices facing the post-colonial leaders are less puzzling than they might seem. They are unequivocal. They must either set up systems which are benevolent or accountable to their citizens for growth and prosperity, or set up unaccountable and repressive systems which are counterproductive. Prior to the East Asian miracle, the conventional wisdom for growth and prosperity was democracy and open market. This is evidently a good state, a combination of open markets and substantial political liberties. The alternative argument was that the unaccountable systems were counterproductive and stifling. The author uses political theory and the prisoner's dilemma to posit the classical theory and its pay-offs in qualitative-terms in figure 1. East Asia showed that the paradox of regulation and open markets could achieve economic goals that are comparable to less restrictive trade and guarantees of political liberty. This situation seems to qualify benevolence as a substitute to repression or lack of accountability when accountability cannot be achieved.

The prisoner's dilemma as used here is representative of the quandary facing some of the post-colonial African states. Political parties seldom want to relinquish political power, because the primary objective of political parties is to capture and maintain political power at all times. In the best state of affairs a political party will be willing to be accountable and relinquish power momentarily if necessary. In the second-best state, it is not willing to relinquish political power, but becomes a goal-oriented dominant party like that of the People's Action Party (PAP) of Singapore. There are institutional structures for some measure of accountability, or the stability to pursue development. In the bad state, political parties are neither positively goal-oriented nor accountable, and they see each other as a threat to their primary goal of capturing political power for limited objectives. A decision is made not to be accountable or positively goal-oriented but to consolidate political power by coercive means for goals that are personal rather than national.

Imagine that there are two political parties in the imaginary Republic of Kaos—the Democratic Corruption Party (DCP), and the National Plutocratic Party (NPP). The upper cells in all quadrants represent the pay-off of choices made by DCP to be accountable or positively goal-oriented and not to be accountable or positively goal-oriented to the citizens of Kaos. The lower cells of all quadrants represent the pay-off of choices made by NPP to be accountable or positively goal-oriented, and not to be accountable or positively goal-oriented to the citizens of Kaos.

The top left-hand quadrant shows that when DCP and NPP are accountable and willing to share political power, momentarily Kaos makes political and economic progress. This is a good state in which both political parties are committed to feedback, reforms, and the general good. The political parties are not isolated from the needs and ambitions of the citizenry. As long as the two parties are positively goal-oriented and committed to accountability and development such a progress would be sustained. The Democratic and Conservative parties of the United States, and the Labor and Conservative Party of Britain exemplify such an argument.

The top right-hand quadrant shows a situation in which NPP is committed to good policy and development because of accountability or positive goal-oriented policies to foster development, but for which the DCP is not committed. In short, it is a mixture of good state and bad state. In the good state, there is progress. If the NPP is removed by a *coup d'état*, or voted out and, therefore, supplanted by a political party which is not positively goal-oriented and resistant to accountability, prior progress becomes transient and it is supplanted by decay. The assumption here is that autocratic parties do not normally campaign on a platform of autocracy to win elections. By deception or chicanery, once in power, such parties normally implement autocratic policies. Without a *coup,* they are therefore voted into power under false pretenses. If the DCP is repressive enough and successful at that for a very long period of time, economic and political decay will be a long-lasting experience. Whatever progress was obtained will be nullified.

If the citizens of Kaos are allowed to keep the NPP for a protracted period of time by their choice, and if the NPP is aware of its potential replacement, progress will be fostered for as long as the NPP is in power. A dominant party like the PAP, which has maintained considerable control of political power since 1959 with a reasonable amount of commitment to growth, exemplifies such a theory.

Figure 1

Prisoner's Dilemma of Political Choices

NPP \ DCP	Accountable	Unaccountable
Accountable	**Progress** / **Progress**	Decay / Progress
Unaccountable	Progress / Decay	**Decay** / **Decay**

Democratic Corruption Party (DCP)
National Plutocratic Party (NPP)

The bottom left-hand quadrant is an inverse of the top right, with a change in the commitment of the political parties involved. If neither party is committed to accountability, and does not pursue positive goal-oriented policies, the outcome is political and economic decay as represented by the lower right quadrant. Most African countries are experiencing decay because of policy failures or their inability to design systems which are stable and accountable. In Sierra Leone, for example, prior to the turn of the twenty-first century, there was no adequate commitment to development by the two major parties. Neither the Sierra Leone People's Party (SLPP) nor the All People's Congress (APC) showed such a commitment. It was more evident however, that both wanted uncontested political hegemony, and tilted more toward corruption and the neglect of policies required for optimal development. Failed states espoused policies which are predictably ruinous.

The *Modus Operandi* of Failed Post-Colonial Leaders

The major causes of African underdevelopment are: political issues associated with lasting one-party rule, military *coups*, corruption, bloated defense expenditures, ethnic exploitation, and civil wars. Corruption is understood by international convention as a legal wrong arising from a particular conduct or activity which suggests the moral bankruptcy of an individual, a bureaucracy or a business.[41]

The uncertainty of the life span of political administration and the mutual distrust of civil administration and military officers normally foster uneasy civil-military relations. The life span of the some African political administration is largely contingent on civil-military relations, and much more recently, the extent to which political leaders could integrate rebel factions into government.

In Sierra Leone, Congo Democratic Republic (CDR), and the Republic of Congo, the struggle for political hegemony continued after independence and civil-military relations complicated the process of conflict resolution. The military became a reinforcing organization of tribal loyalty, which was perceived to be essential for the preservation of political power. This was an unfortunate policy which was never intended to correct one of the most poignant criticisms of colonialism, divide and rule/conquer.

The leadership of Albert Margai and the SLPP is much noted for the transparent use of tribalism to gratify his *Mende* supporters from the south. Virtually, every vacancy in the civil-service and the armed forces were filled by his tribesmen in the early 1960s. Yet, such a policy was a political casualty which contradicts the realistic expectations of democracy. The capture of political power by democratic means inevitably necessitates widespread support. Parochialism or tribalism is divisive politics, which merely alienate and infuriate the marginalized segment of society with no guarantee that it would appease all of those it is intended to protect or benefit. The success of such a policy is dependent on how best democracy can be sacrificed to authoritarianism. This was, in actual fact, what enticed the early politicians to the fatal attraction of the one-party system. This idea was avidly conceived and pursued feverishly by Albert Margai, but it was brought to fruition by Siaka Stevens. Cox captures the one-party sentiment of the age:

> Even Sir Albert's sympathy with a single-party regime, especially after October 1965, reflected not a commitment by certain members by the ruling party to an abstract concept but rather the desire of the SLPP leaders and chiefs to protect their special class and personal interest against subversion by the more populist APC.[42]

Indeed, the *nouveau riche* and newly formed élitist class were quick in their desire to subvert the bourgeoning democratic process. Albert Margai surreptitiously plotted the preservation of his political power, which also meant the gradual destruction of viable alternative political parties. For example, he cajoled Paramount Chiefs to support the SLPP and by tacit insinuation dare them to campaign for an alternative party.

A member of parliament once recounted an utterance of the visibly power-crazed political leader. "I have all the power… I am standing here by the hill with my bren gun and people hold machetes to come and fight me. I shall kill them *baybayraybay* [in large quantities]"[43] The logical extension of this desire to hold on to power meant cooperation with the military—a politicization of the army at the inception of independence. With time, the army came to see itself as privileged and indispensable to civilian politics. Indeed, the civil war, which overtook Sierra Leone for approximately ten years in the late twentieth to early twenty-first century, may be partly attributed to the challenge of this military presumption. Officers must be wooed or courted for the preservation of civilian regimes, not alienated or disbanded. Convincing support went beyond the realm of wooing and courting into the domain of tribal loyalty and support, an insurance policy to latch on to political power without having an undesirable *coup d'état.*

In Sierra Leone, as the political elites or civilian executives fraternized with the senior military officers and pandered to the military, the civil politicians were able to maintain a nexus. This nexus was facilitated by the rapid Africanization of the military to obtain a political objective of pacification. Cox observes that, between May 1964 and March 1967 during the tenure of Albert Margai's leadership, a truly Sierra Leonean army became a distinct reality. This could be contrasted to the approximately sixteen British officers on secondment out of a-fifty man officer establishment at the death of the prior leader. David Lansana, who assumed command of the regiment, became a close associate of Albert Margai and the inner core of the SLPP. Of the nine most senior officers of the army, seven belonged to extended families.[44]

The association of Lansana (a *Mende* by tribe) with Albert Margai (also a *Mende*) and the SLPP subsequently played a pivotal role in the change of political leadership with long-lasting ramifications. There were other *Mendes* of prominence in the army—Major Ambrose Genda, Captain Bockarie Kai-Samba, and Captain Sandi Jumu. *Mende* preeminence could be attributed to numerous and high quality schools in the south compared to the north, but the systematic and deliberate policy of exclusion makes it difficult to fend off the appearance and realism of tribalism. In actual fact, the harbingers of western civilization had been the European missionaries and the *Creoles*. In both civil and military positions of leadership, non-*Mendes* were carefully weeded out.

The Africanization of the military and the new role which the military was supposed to play in civilian politics ushered in the dawn of military corruption and the propensity of the military to capture political power and rule as civilians rather than staying in the barracks—a radicalization of the perspective and focus of the military, subsequently compounded by a breakdown of discipline.

The army was splintered into camps as it became infected by politics. Morale among senior officers was low and the favoritism which informed the Brigadier's conflict management skills earned him very little respect among his peers. He was already a bag full of political and military liabilities.

By 1967, the Prime Minister, Albert Margai, became unsecured and concerned about *coup* plots. What seemed to be frivolous charges or baseless accusations, were intended to charge suspect officers and politicians with treason for the preservation of his government. The Margai government had other plans which unraveled themselves in blatant corruption and personal enrichment of some of the SLPP elites. Reserves of the Sierra Leone Produce Marketing Board

(SLPMB) were squandered. Diamonds were illicitly trafficked and ill-gotten wealth was amassed. As early as 1966, the International Monetary Fund (IMF) had been summoned for help with stabilization.

The anomalies and fraud provided the APC a platform on which to run for the 1967 elections—SLPP self-enrichment, mismanagement of a fragile economy, and *Mende* favoritism. Ironically, the APC subsequently perfected the mismanagement and gave the concept of the one-party state finality. As the SLPP struggled to patch its platform and paper over the cracks, the APC was gratuitously fed unsolicited substance with which to defeat the SLPP.

The SLPP was clearly in trouble and the 1967 elections were conducted with multiple incidents. The conditions for crises had already been fomented. The military had already been groomed to be the gadfly of corrupt politicians, but by the start of 1967, the date for the elections was not readily apparent. The government was to later announce that elections would be held on March 17, 1967, for sixty-six ordinary seats, and March 21, 1967, for the twelve Paramount Chiefs. What had been an emerging democracy was in peril.

The Margai government amended the Electoral Provisions Act to raise the deposit made by candidates from Le 200 to Le 500. Almost immediately, there was an inclination towards a plutocratic system. The Electoral Commission was also flawed with indications of favoritism and impropriety, and contrary to constitutional provision, Section 37(8) officers of the commission were first approved by the Prime Minister. Although the elections went on with unusual calm, the results were generally unknown three days later. Shortly thereafter the Governor-General, Sir Henry Lightfoot-Boston, tried to broker a power sharing deal between the APC and SLPP, which the APC stalwarts rejected.

On March 21, 1967, the Governor-General used his constitutional power to appoint Siaka Stevens as Prime Minister of Sierra Leone, much to the chagrin of Lansana who had forewarned against an exercise of power. Just as Stevens was about to be sworn in as Prime Minister, the ceremony was interrupted by a military junta under the direction of Lansana, who called the ceremony "unconstitutional." The army took control later that day under the pretext of being custodian of state security. If the army had not intervened, Sierra Leone would have been an example of the first peaceful transfer of political power in Independent Africa, with a propensity to nurture democratic principles.

The presumption of the military established a dangerous precedent for subsequent civil-military relations. For the next twenty-four years, conventional wisdom suggested that a civilian administration cannot function well without integrating the military into civilian politics. In fact, such an unholy alliance reinforced the illegitimate regime of Stevens and his APC stalwarts for almost two decades.

The Lansana *coup* was short-lived as another supposedly more popular junta wrested power from him shortly after his seizure of power. The counter-*coup* soldiers eventually formed themselves into the National Reformation Council (NRC) under the chairmanship of Lieutenant Colonel Juxon Smith. It became less apparent later that one of the motives of the Lansana *coup* was to protect his ally, Albert Margai, from accountability for maladministration and corruption. A much more sympathetic leader from the south would have been capable of doing just that. This nascent republic was already conversant with political policies of corruption and nepotism, which obviously had severe economic consequences. The economic malaise manifested itself in the form of an economic crisis which emanated from defalcation and corruption in high places. The Sierra Leone Produce Marketing Board (SLPMB), one of the primary sources of revenue, was badly damaged, and with that the fortunes of agriculture. A similar policy of concerted corruption to consolidate political power was also found in the CDR.

Like Albert Margai, Mobutu consolidated power by sharing national wealth with political allies. Millions of dollars in western aid, typical of Cold War competition for African friendship or alliance, vanished into thin air. Export earnings generated by diamond exports were vastly siphoned and unaccounted for. It is believed that by the 1980s, Mobutu had amassed fraudulent wealth to the tune of about $4 billion, and as the Cold War ended, the United States cut direct aid to Mobutu's regime.

Between 1967 and 1991, Sierra Leone witnessed at least five *coups d'état*, which ultimately culminated in a civil war for more than a decade. The *coups* indicated here were not necessarily reflective of potential or failed ones. Table 3.1 gives the sequence or timing of such *coups*. *Coups* and wars have become the logical offshoot of adverse political policies.

The CDR and the Sudan have spent the greater part of the twentieth century fighting wars and diverting substantial and valuable resources to the prosecution of such wars. The CDR became independent in 1960, the year before independence was granted to Sierra Leone, but there was no time to savor the attainment of independence. In that same year, army mutinies occurred and the President, Joseph Kasavubu, was already fighting with his Prime Minister, Patrice Lumumba, who was eventually arrested in 1960, and assassinated in 1961. The fighting in the CDR was multi-faceted, and involved the secessionist movement of the diamond rich province of *Katanga* pioneered by Moise Tshombe. Tshombe was appointed Prime Minister in 1964 to replace Lumumba, but both the President and Prime Minister were ousted by a military *coup* in 1965.

The officer who was responsible for the *coup*, Joseph Mobutu, and who was to rule for more than three decades, wasted no time to consolidate his new political acquisition. He nationalized many foreign owned-firms between 1973 and 1974, and ran European investors out of the country to affirm his aggrandizement. This type of policy has not been found to be atypical of radical anti-imperialist sentiments. It took him about three years to reverse the policy, but a much longer time to realize the absurdity of the one-party system. Yet Mobutu maintained a chokehold over his opponents until he was deposed in 1997 by Laurent-Desire Kabila, who proved to be equally autocratic.

Table 3.1
Coups d'état and civil wars in CDR, Congo Republic, Sierra Leone, and Sudan.

Country	1958	60	63/4	65	67	68	69	71	72
CDR		+		+w					
Congo Rep			+			+			
Sierra Leone					+	+			
Sudan	+		+w	w	w		+w	+w	w

Country	1974	76/77	85	89	91	92	93	97	04
CDR							wf	w	wf
Congo Rep		+					+w	+w	
Sierra Leone	f	f			w	+w	w	+w	
Sudan		f	+w	+w	w	w	w	w	w

w: Indicates civil wars; wars were fought in some years which have been excluded after their commencement.
f: Indicates years for which *coups* failed. Failed attempts are not always captured credibly and some are not considered.
+: Symbolizes successful *coups*.

The country's vast potential, under the Mobutu regime was thwarted by widespread corruption, economic controls, and the diversion of public resources for personal gain. The unrecorded and illicit transactions of Zaire's unofficial economy were estimated in the early 1990s to be three times the size of official GDP (Bureau of African Affairs).

During the mid twentieth century and immediately after independence, Table 3.1 shows that collectively, on average after every three to four years there was a probability of executing a *coup d'état* (successful or not) or engaging in some kind of war. Such an interval is about the required amount of time for political parties to seek fresh mandate from the voters in democratic societies. By the turn of the twenty-first century, each and every one of the countries proved to be incompetent to deal with the vestiges of colonial rule and was deeply involved in a civil war.

In 1968, civilian government was restored in Sierra Leone under the leadership of Siaka Stevens. It is obvious that Stevens learnt how to safeguard and implement the unaccomplished vices of the SLPP. By the end of the Stevens administration, Sierra Leone was a republic. The economy had been mismanaged, and a one party state was established. Corruption stunk to high heaven. In short, there was little or no marginal improvement for economic growth. What was noticeably incremental was a modest increase in a sense of nationalism, which is always a welcomed idea to building a cohesive state.

The arguments that are generally made for the construction of the one-party state are transparently disingenuous but convenient. Two concepts are ostensibly and ironically used to justify the adoption of the one-party state in the post-colonial era—anti-imperialism and nationalism. Neither of these concepts has formed a sincere basis for any practical or meaningful policy in these countries. First, it is hard to find the severed relationships with the so-called "imperialists." Is imperialism a code word for capitalism? If yes, to what extent have the post-colonial regimes been socialist anyway? Second, these countries have been exposed to more "ethnic wars" than any period under colonialism in terms of severity or duration.

Some of the African leaders who shared strong anti-imperialist feelings, like Lumumba of the CDR, were fully aware of the fundamental obstacle to the riddance of colonialism—ethnic rivalry. Some others were evidently oblivious of the challenge, but they saw anti-imperialist sentiments as a convenient medium to prolonging their stay in power and receiving competing financial aid from capitalist and socialist societies alike. In the Republic of Congo, Alphonse Massembe-Débat instituted a Marxist-Leninist government shortly after independence in 1960, but he was overthrown in 1968. His successor, Maj Marien Ngouabi, made no radical departure from a socialist regime until his assassination in 1975. In 1990, there was a realization that the one-party state was inimical to economic progress, but, by 2002, the country reversed itself and resorted to the persecution of opponents under Sassou-Nguesso.

In the Sudan, regional and religious issues have plagued the state since colonial administration, and they were exacerbated by the colonial territorial delineation prior to independence. The North has repeatedly tried to Arabize, Islamize, and enslave the predominantly Christian African south, and, by so doing, has laid the basis for an ever-present *casus belli*.

The military *coups* of the mid and late 1960s were partly an effort to deal with constitutional problems involving factionalism, economic decay, and ethnic rivalry. The leader of the 1969 *coup*, Colonel Gaafar Muhhamad Numeri, called for the adoption of socialism and the renunciation of all political parties as a pre-condition for southern autonomy. The proposal was promptly rebuffed by the south.

Marxist and non-Marxist sentiments played a crucial rule in the contagion and succession of *coups* in the Sudan in the 1970s. For example, in 1971, the Sudanese Communist Party (SCP) deposed the Numeri regime, but, several days later, a counter-*coup* by the anti-communists restored Numeri. About five years later a bloody but unsuccessful *coup* attempt was made on the Numeri regime.

In 1985, drought and famine broke out in the Sudan in addition to fuel shortage. The Sudan People's Liberation Movement (SPLM) and its military complement, the Sudan People's Liberation Army (SPLA) were formed with the declared objective of achieving a secular, democratic and pluralistic Sudan. By and large, the struggle in the Sudan is consistent with the causes of secessionist movements in Sierra Leone, Nigeria, and the Congo Democratic Republic (CDR).

The Sudan has failed to implement a cohesive policy to address regional differences. Policies are more often than not intended to marginalize the south, deprive the south of basic rights, or exclude the south from policies which are perceived as national. The logical effect of the anomaly is the demand for the right of political participation or autonomy. The impasse causes war in the absence of a political solution. The situation became much worse by the turn of the 1980s when the state moved toward a theocracy when the *Shari'a* was incorporated into the penal code.

Wars generally have economic consequences, one of which is the diversion of limited resources to their prosecution. Ironically, the amount of resources that has been set aside to finance military expenditure as a percentage of government expenditure in the African countries is equally as large as that of the US, if not greater than that of the US.[45]

The post colonial state showed little appetite for political tolerance or the diffusion of political or economic power to deal with either the havoc of balkanization, or the delineation of boundaries which they inherited. The one-party state, or the inability to accommodate civil opposition and implement growth oriented policies, has become an unmitigated disaster. The propaganda for the adoption of the one party system in Sierra Leone was deliberate and massive. The A.P.C. writes:

> Anti-imperialism also played a part in creating a mood receptive to the one-party idea. The multi-party system was seen as part of the British legacy, imposed on Sierra Leoneans willy-nilly as a condition for independence, despite the fact that Britain tolerated no opposition to her own rule and had done nothing prior to 1951 to introduce the concept of parties to Sierra Leone...the one-party state represented an attempt to recover this idealized golden age of innocencc . It was in line with this sort of thinking that President Stevens called the one-party state "the abolition of a political system inherited from British colonialists and...its replacement by one more in tune with our Sierra Leonean and African heritage". The concept of a 'loyal opposition'—that late eighteenth century English concept which is so essential to western multi-party systems—was particularly alien in Sierra Leone. [46]

Prior to the adoption of the one-party constitution in 1978, the dominant political party in Sierra Leone, the APC, was already floundering, but Stevens had already planned a constitutional scheme for a life-long possession of political power which was intolerant of opposition, loyal or not. Constitutional reforms were a way of fine-tuning the much more blatant decrees of the likes of Bokassa. The United Democratic Party (UDP), which broke away from the APC, was, in fact, a splinter of the APC, a breakaway group of the APC which was opposed to the tendency to establish personal rule.

Mobutu shared the one-party notions of Stevens. In 1970, he established the Popular Movement of the Revolution (MPR) as the sole political party. Anti-imperialist sentiments were demonstrated by a growing sense of Africanization. The change of nomenclature and personnel more than anything else exemplified the Africanization process for Mobutu. The CDR was to be renamed Zaire in 1971, the supposedly true local name of the Congo River. Mobutu was to be called *Mobutu Sese Seko Kuku Ngbendu wa Banga* ("the all powerful warrior who, because of his endurance and inflexible will to win, will go from conquest to conquest leaving fire in his wake").[47]

In the Central African Republic (CAR), which was part of the Federation of French Equatorial Africa, the implementation of the one-party state was rapid. In 1958, the territory obtained independence with Boganda as prime minister. The rule of Boganda, like that of Milton Margai of Sierra Leone, was brief. Boganda died the following year, and Milton Margai died in 1964, three years later after independence. David Dacko, the nephew of Boganda, took over as President of CAR in 1960, and, within two years, the state was declared a one-party state with MESAN as the sole political party. He was subsequently ousted by Jean-Bedel Bokassa, his army commander, who in 1972, declared himself president for life.

After three decades of political and economic crises, the four countries (Sierra Leone, CDR, the Republic of Congo, and the Sudan) have engaged in intermittent and protracted civil wars. People normally will not fight because of basic ethnic differences, but because of some underlying and fundamental deprivation that is based on a perceived sense of injustice. These might be the deprivation of food, income, education, health, wealth, the right to live freely, or just the right to have a political or religious opinion which might be different or unique. Ironically these are the rights that humanize the human being as a person, and they are normally to be found in the entrenched clauses of the constitutions of the post-colonial states. They are, otherwise, known as "inalienable" rights or rights which are unimpeachable. The economic consequences of bad post-colonial political choices will be discussed in the next chapter.

Reversing the Ills of Colonialism—an East Asian Miracle

Over the years, it has been fashionable to argue that the former colonial societies of Africa are backward and underdeveloped because of their experience with colonialism. Although this theory cannot be entirely debunked and could be ascribed some merits because of the failures of colonialism, it is an inadequate explanation for crisis and underdevelopment in post-colonial Africa. Evidence suggests that the adoption of sound political policy after independence diminishes the viability of the colonial theory as an explanation of underdevelopment.

Singapore makes a compelling case for an alternative theory to that of colonialism.

Singapore, like most of the African colonies, became a crown colony on April 1, 1867, approximately fifty-nine years later than Sierra Leone. The Crown Colony system of government or its structure in Singapore was consistent with the one used in Africa. The Executive Council included the Governor, the senior military official and other senior officials. The Legislative Council consisted of the members of the Executive Council, the Chief Justice, and non-official members nominated by the Governor. This is largely the typical microcosm of the British fusion of powers that was used to administer British colonies.

Unlike Sierra Leone, the CDR, the Republic of Congo, and Sudan; Singapore is not well endowed with the natural resources of gold, diamonds, iron ore, piassava, copper, zinc, or oil. Its primary source of revenue comes from commerce and its fishing industry, which could be attributed to its strategic location on the Indian Ocean. It acts as an entrepôt for the resources of Malay, and it facilitates the disembarkation of Chinese, Indians, Indonesians, Malays, and others, *en route* to other countries of the world. Singapore became a major port for ships moving between Europe and East Asia. As rubber planting boomed after the 1870s, it became an important sorting and export centre in the world for rubber trade, and, by the end of the nineteenth century, it was already a very prosperous colony. Peace and prosperity were thwarted with the advent of the Second World War. In December 1941, Singapore fell under Japanese control for about three years, after which it was recaptured by the British.

Like most of the African states, Singapore is cosmopolitan. Its religious composition consists of Buddhists, Muslims, Christians, Hindus, Taoists, Sikhs, and Confucians. Chinese, Malays and Indians form the dominant ethnic groups. Colonial administration and the movement to Independence were equally troublesome.

The colonial regime provided little or no opportunities for local participation, but, by the end of the war, there was a radical change in the attitude of the British toward political participation. The people of Singapore, mostly the enlightened and business classes, demanded more participation in government just like the Africans.

The Executive and Legislative Councils maintained a tight hold over power with the Governor retaining a firm control over the colony. Unlike the modest reforms that had been made in Sierra Leone as far back as 1922 when the Slatter Constitution was introduced, provision for the election of six members to the Legislative Council by popular vote in Singapore took place in March 1948. After an abortive rebellion by the Communist Party of Malaya, the British government declared a state of emergency, and it was not until the end of 1953 that the British government appointed a commission under Sir George Rendel to review Singapore's constitutional position and to make recommendations for change.

When the Communist Party of Malaya tried to take over Malaya and Singapore by force, a state of emergency was declared in June 1948. The emergency lasted for 12 years. The Rendel proposals were accepted by the government by the end of 1953 and they served as the basis of a new constitution that gave Singapore a greater measure of self-government.

As the Colonial Office contemplated the independence of Singapore in the mid 1950s, it originally decided on the formation of a Malayan union which would include all the Malay states, Penang, and Malacca with Singapore as the headquarters of the British Governor-General for Southeast Asia. At independence, Singapore was to be administered separately as an entity unto itself.

It is not too clear why the British entertained such a plan, which was an unusual deviation from the colonial policy of amalgamation in Africa. For example, in Sierra Leone, and the Sudan, there were pointed arguments for the secession of territories but the British opposed the separation of protectorate from colony. Many of the business classes and colonial officials were in opposition to a plan of separating Singapore from the Malayan peninsula. In September 1945, Singapore became the headquarters for the British Military Administration (BMA).

The first major election in Singapore was held in 1955. The Labor Front won ten seats. The PAP, which had four candidates, won three seats, and David Marshall of the Labor Front became Singapore's first Chief Minister on April 6, 1955. A coalition government made up of the Labor Front, the United Malays National Organization, and the Malayan Chinese Association was formed. On May 28, 1958, a Constitutional Agreement was signed in London that was to lead to eventual independence. Self-government was attained in 1959.

The first general election to a fully-elected Legislative Assembly of fifty-one representatives was held in 1959. The PAP won forty-three seats, which is about 53.4 percent of the total votes cast. On June 3, the new constitution, which confirmed Singapore as a self-governing state, was brought into force, and the first Government of the State of Singapore was headed by PAP's Lee Kuan Yew, Singapore's first Prime Minister.

The independence movement in Singapore was not spectacularly different from the challenges that confronted the Africans. Independence movement necessitates coalition building, a sense of nationalism, which is crucial to minimizing setbacks of colonialism. Within coalitions are divergent interests and aspirations. Often times, some of these differences seem irreconcilable, and it takes prudence and persuasion to achieve a consensus or compromise. The PAP obtained power because of a united front with the communists. What unified these rival parties more than anything else was their resolution to fight and subjugate British colonialism. However, development requires more than the expulsion of colonial rulers.

The communists controlled many mass organizations, especially of workers and students. It was apparent that the alliance between the PAP moderates and the pro-communists was a tenuous one, with each party trying to attain its objective at the expense of the other—a dichotomous situation in which communists tip-toed around the idea of accommodating non-communists, and vice-versa. Tension between the two factions worsened from 1960 to 1961, leading to disintegration. The pro-communists formed a new political party, the *Barisan Sosialis*. There were other differences in the nascent nation, which included the status of Singapore, and the control of foreign affairs, internal security, and defense of Singapore.

The Malayan Prime Minister, Tunku (Tengku) Abdul Rahman, proposed closer political and economic co-operation between the Federation of Malaya, Singapore, Sarawak, North Borneo and Brunei in the form of a merger. He was able to forge a consensus with Lee Kuan Yew. The central government was to be responsible for the defense, foreign affairs and internal security, but matters pertaining to education and labor were to be left in the realm of local autonomy. A 1962 referendum showed overwhelming support for the merger and the PAP's plan to implement the merger. On September 16, 1963, Malaysia was formed, consisting of the Federation of Malaya, Singapore, Sarawak and North Borneo/Sabah. Opponents of the union included: Brunei, Indonesian President, Sukarno, and the Philippines.

The union proved to be problematic. Sukarno severed diplomatic and trade relations between Indonesia and Malaysia. The economic sanctions were intended to cripple the economy of the union. Singapore was hard hit. Indonesian commandos conducted armed raids into Sabah and Sarawak, and Singaporean fishing boats were seized by Indonesian gunboats. Indonesian propaganda was intended to rile up Singapore Malays and arouse ethnic animosities. Singapore Malays had hoped that the union would provide them identical opportunities for employment and obtaining licenses that were given to the Malays of the Federation. The PAP government granted no extra economic benefits to the Singapore Malays, but provided financial aid for education. Interference from extremist elements of the Malaysian United Malays National Organization (UMNO) and the confrontational attitude of Sukarno led to ethnic and racial riots in Singapore by 1964.

The racist upheaval in Singapore was dramatic and shocking for a country that had prided itself on racial harmony. Yet, its outburst is an indication of the cancer in post-colonial societies. This is most evident in the African societies where ethnicity has been used to solidify political bases, as much as to prosecute internecine wars.

The Singapore situation was doleful for other reasons. The first year of unification proved to be a financial disaster. The hopes of a common market were dashed, and Kuala Lumpur demanded a higher percentage of Singapore's revenue to offset the defense expenditures incurred as a result of fighting against hostilities. There were also punitive threats of closing the Bank of China, which handled trade arrangements and remittances between Singapore and China.

Political tension and mutual distrust arose over interference in domestic elections as candidates in Kuala Lumpur gained support from Singapore and vice-versa. One of the visible results of the intrusions was the formation of alliances of political movements or parties to reflect opposing interests in each polity. For example, in 1965, four alliance parties of Malaya, Singapore, Sabah, and Sarawak merged to form a Malaysian National Alliance Party. The following month there was retaliation in Singapore. PAP and four opposition parties from Malaya and Sarawak formed the Malaysian Solidarity Convention whose members were ethnic Chinese. Singapore represented a polity, in which as much as Sierra Leone, post-colonial party formation was predominantly based on ethnic and business ties. It would be recalled, for example, that the SLPP of Sierra Leone was dominated by *Mendes*; the National Council of the Colony of Sierra Leone (NCCSL/NC), by *Creoles*; and the APC, by *Temnes* from the North. The Singapore-Malaya merger was destined to fail.

Mindful of the evolving events, a stinging literary war, and the potential for unrest, Tunku Abdul Rahman decided to separate Singapore from Malaysia, but not before the call for the arrest of Lee Kuan Yew and other PAP leaders by UMNO extremists. What happened in Singapore prior to deliberate policy decisions actually mirrored the post-colonial political turmoil in Africa at the dawn of independence.

On August 9, 1965, Singapore was separated from Malaya, and Lee declared Singapore a sovereign democratic and independent state that same day. The independent Singapore was admitted to the United Nations on September 21, 1965, and it became a member of the Commonwealth of Nations on October 15, 1965.

The separation of Singapore from Malaya meant formidable challenges for Singapore. Singapore was heavily dependent on Malayan tin, rubber, and other important articles of trade, partly because it has inadequate natural resources of its own. Second, most of Singapore's political leaders were Malayan-born with ties to Malaya.[48] The struggle for Singapore's survival, like that of the former colonial African countries, started in the mid 1960s.

Singapore's strategy for survival and development was essentially to forge unity, and take advantage of its strategic location on the Indian Ocean. This involved resolving the ethnic fracases associated with colonialism and the decolonization process, and using geography to make up for inadequate natural resources.

The post-colonial state urgently sought to create a "Singaporean identity." A Constitutional Commission on Minority Rights was created in 1965 and an official policy was developed to encourage ethnic and cultural diversity. The goal of the government was oriented toward the creation of a lasting melting pot. In 1965 the Foreign Minister, Rajaratnam, informed the United Nations (UN) General Assembly that if Singapore could stick to a policy of national unification for the next thirty years, Singapore would be able to create a man rooted in the cultures of four great civilizations but not belonging exclusively to any of them.[49]

Educational institutions and public housing became trajectories for the delivery of the official policy of integration. Integrated schools and public housing became the primary facilities for the combination of various ethnic groups. Modern high-rise housing estates and new towns provided avenues for interaction, and indigenous languages were taught to reflect cultural awareness but not at the expense of a national identity.

Anti-corruption and economic policies went hand in hand with nation building. The government launched an anti-corruption campaign at all levels of its administration. A largely graft-free government, skilled workforce, and efficient infrastructure attracted investments from the US, Japan and Europe. Transnationals accounted for more than two-thirds of manufacturing output and direct export sales. For countries lacking significant savings, long-term foreign investment is particularly crucial to augmenting savings.

Unlike Singapore, the African countries did not register adequate successes with long-term foreign direct investment as a net inflow percent of GDP. With very few exceptions, the 1980s were particularly bad for foreign direct investment in the African countries. This era witnessed the debt crisis, which impeded growth through the lack of foreign investment, or the inefficiency of investment. Substantial work has been done to draw attention to the implications of savings and investment, the problems associated with debt, and methods to reduce debts. For example, Krugman, 1989; Sachs, 1990; Borensztein, 1990; Bosworth and Collins, 1999; and Pattillo, Ricci and Poirson in 2002. The argument that debt discourages investment is variously known in economic literature as the "debt overhang" argument. The ability of the Singapore government to keep corruption and debt in check provided bigger gains not only for the attraction of foreign capital, but also in achieving the export-oriented goal of the government.

When the hopes of developing a common market with Malaysia were dashed, the government focused on in-sourcing, a strategy of attracting foreign capital to stimulate export oriented industries and to reduce reliance on Britain as a major source of investment capital. Singapore promoted trade with the US and Japan and it later promoted trade with Indonesia after the strained relationship was patched in the late 1960s. International trade formed the backbone of the economy. Five sectors were deemed to be specifically crucial: regional entrepôt trade; manufacturing; petroleum refining and shipping; production of goods and services for the domestic economy; and specialized banking and finance.

The export-oriented strategy of the government combined state-directed investments in strategic government-owned enterprises with foreign investment. Government owned enterprises are normally used to maintain some amount of flexibility, and facilitate, or reinforce growth-oriented policies. For example, in 1986, the Singapore Broadcasting Corporation formed a subsidiary to produce commercials on a fee-for-service basis. Many state and quasi-state companies were created by ministries or organized under government holding companies like Temasek or the Sheng-Li Holding Company, which provided a wide range of goods and services. The government also participated in joint ventures, which involved steel and sugar industries, and the National Trades Union Congress (NTUC) ran cooperative businesses including supermarkets, and traveling.

The economic policies of the Singapore government contributed to an average Gross Domestic Product (GDP) growth of about 8.5 percent for four decades.[50] This can be contrasted to Sierra Leone's approximate rate of 1.13 percent; CDR's, 0.18 percent; Republic of Congo's 4 percent; the Sudan's 3.4 percent; or the US' 3.4 percent in Tables 3 to 7 respectively. It could also be seen that while Singapore was averaging about 9 percent GDP growth in the 1960s and 1970s, its counterparts were averaging 4 percent or less. Latin American states, which were preoccupied with neo-colonialist theories and Import Substitution, were equally unable to outperform Singapore. Brazil's growth rate of per capita GDP as a share of regional GDP between 1950 and 1980 averaged about 4.2 percent. That of Mexico was 3.0 and Argentina 1.8. The 1980s were particularly bad, with largely negative GDP per capita growth rates for the region.[51] Export-driven growth, with some measure of protection, proved to be advantageous for Singapore; at least in the sense of not overprotecting inefficient industries, but it challenged them to be more skillful, competitive, and productive. Pushing export and freeing up trade was a winning strategy for Singapore; a curious mix of intervention and freedom (managed trade).[52]

Singapore's imports of goods and services as a percentage of GDP in the 1960's and 1970s were evidently greater than exports, but, by the end of the 1980s, it began to reap the benefits of prior imports that were intended to stimulate its export capacity. For Sierra Leone, the CDR, and the Sudan, imports of goods and services as a percentage of GDP have consistently been greater. This was the case for the Republic of Congo until the 1980s and 1990s.

After Britain pulled out from their naval bases in the late 1960s, the government of Singapore called for an election to deal with what seemed like a looming crisis for defense and unemployment. The bases were eventually converted to economic assets for commerce and industry. Structurally unemployed workers were re-trained for new jobs befitting the new paradigm for economic growth and prosperity. The former colonial George VI Graving Dock was converted to the Sembawang Shipyard to repair and build ships, and, by 1972, the country became the container transshipment center of Southeast Asia. By the mid 1970s, Singapore became the world's third busiest port following Rotterdam and New York.[53]

The economic changes targeted employment, and labor laws sought a balance between the interests of workers and employers. The post-colonial period witnessed fractious labor relations, which ranged from hostility to PAP as espoused by the left-wing Singapore Association of Trade Unions (SATU), to some form of consensus with the PAP, exemplified by the noncommunist National Trades Union Congress (NTUC). As in various areas of Africa, trade unions were a principal instrument in the anti-colonial struggle. In Singapore, they were used both by the democratic socialist PAP and the communists with whom they cooperated uneasily. However, the government worked around the discontents to obtain meaningful labor reforms.

Workers were made to work longer hours, but they were provided sick leave and unemployment compensation. Employers were obligated to increase their contributions to the Central Provident Fund (CPF). This fund became essential to home ownership and savings. Singaporeans were allowed to use their CPF savings to pay for apartments or own homes, but government motivated savings also provided reserves to tide over Singaporeans in economic downturns (attributed to exogenous changes), and finance long-term national projects.

The government focused on hi-tech industries and the skilled work force necessary to meet that challenge. The skilled work force was essential to attract more international investment. As a result of the economic and political reforms, productivity increased considerably and Singapore enjoyed a remarkable level of employment. The dependence on international trade made the economic performance of Singapore to be highly contingent on exogenous factors. The countervailing measures were therefore largely perceived of in terms of the management of savings, the factors of production, and productivity.

Productivity has much to do with the amount of goods and services produced during a period of time (usually one hour), and is normally reflective of the know-how in the process. Its positive net effect is to increase output and reduce cost in the process of production. A standard growth model captures productivity in terms of what cannot be explained by the inputs of capital and labor. Although the unexplained was once considered to be a residual by Solow, it is largely attributed to technological progress, education or the behavior of governments today:

$$\Delta A/A = \Delta Y/Y - \alpha \Delta K/K - (1\text{-}\alpha)\Delta L/L;$$

where $\Delta A/A$ is growth in total factor productivity; $\alpha\Delta K/K$ is the contribution of capital; and $(1\text{-}\alpha)\Delta L/L$ is the contribution of labor. The share of output attributed to capital and labor is α, and $(1\text{-}\alpha)$ respectively. The sum of these add up to one, and, therefore, a production function, $Y = AK^{\alpha}\ L^{(1-\alpha)}$ which exhibits constant returns to scale in its capital augmenting form.

The average rate of unemployment as a percent of the total labor force in the 1980s for example, was 3.52, which subsequently dropped to an average of 2.75 in the 1990s. These rates were significantly lower than those of the US. The values for the African countries are unobtainable. Low levels of inflation generally complemented low levels of unemployment, except for the 1970s, which was marked by the oil crisis, when the annual percentage change of consumer prices fluctuated between one and two percent in approximate terms. Annual inflation rates of change for the African countries in tables 3.2-3.6 have galloped significantly. The prosperity in Singapore was not to be squandered by population growth or explosion. In 1966, the government launched a family planning program to keep population in check.

Control of population proved to be effective. For two decades, the rates of growth were kept lower than the average for the 1960s. The average growth rate of per capita GDP was also consistently higher than that of population since the 1960s. This is also true for the US. For Sierra Leone, this was true only in the 1960s, and was never the case for the other African countries in the tables.

Industrial estates sprung up. By the late 1970s, at least 271 factories were already in existence, and more than 100 factories were under construction. Unemployment fell and immigration laws were made less stringent to accommodate labor shortages. What was once an impoverished, colonized, and strife-torn country of the late 1940s was set on a path to growth and prosperity by the end of the 1970s when most of its African counterparts were still struggling with corruption, political instability, lack of nationalism, and growth oriented commitment. What is largely perceived as a miracle (high performance) is in reality the result of realpolitik. This is a second best country, which traded off effective opposition in favor of growth-oriented policies that combined openness with a dominant government—a curious blend of free market and regulation. Prosperity came through the machinations of a dominant party, the PAP.[54] It may be worthwhile to contrast this puzzling blend of regulation and market, which traded off some civil rights for growth and prosperity, with the repudiation of civil rights in Africa which provided no positive externalities.

The government of Singapore exercised wide discretionary power, which limited the liberties of its citizens through what might seem to be judicious means. For example, government leaders utilized court proceedings and defamation suits against political opponents and critics. These suits, which more often than not, have been decided in favor of government plaintiffs, have muzzled political speech and action, and they created a perception that the ruling party used the judicial system for political purposes. After the 2001 general election, Senior Minister Lee Kuan Yen and Prime Minister Goh Chok Tong sued an opposition leader, Chee Soon Juan, for defamation based on comments Chee made during the campaign. In August, a court ordered a hearing to set the amount of damages Chee would owe the Ministers. Despite the legal wranglings between the government and opponents, Singapore continues to grow.

Singapore, which had laid a basis for growth and development in the 1960s, continues to enjoy a robust growth at the turn of the twenty-first century. Singapore's growth and prosperity could be largely attributed to deliberate policies geared towards savings, low inflation and full employment, political stability, efficient administration, skilled labor/productivity, and regional peace. The obvious failure of some African countries to deal with primordial ethnic differences conciliatorily, and chart growth-oriented policies set them on the path of underdevelopment. Going forward, it is evident that the changing circumstances in the global economy are not likely to facilitate an easy recovery of the lost decades. For example, in the past less stringent rules allowed for more export subsidies, tax credits and unfair trade practices.

For African countries which squandered growth opportunities and continue to wage wars, the going is likely to get tougher unless there is a sense of urgency and change of direction from corruption and internecine wars, to providing a skilled workforce, attaining political stability, checking population growth, and increasing national savings and productivity. The absence of a sense of urgency in the 1960s, lack of well focused policies, and international co-operation with fraudulent regimes, have constituted preconditions for crises and underdevelopment.

Table 3.2

*Economic indicators, **Singapore**, 1960s-1990s*

Year	GDP (pc)	Military Sp	Imp	Ex	Debt Svc	pop	FDI	unemp	Inf
1960s	6.99[a]	x	131[b]	121[c]	x	2.6	x	x	1.2[e]
1970s	7.73	x	156	145	x	1.5	5.8[d]	x	5.9
1980s	5.22	x	191	190	x	2.1	10	3.52	2.8
1990s	4.51	21.86	164	164	x	3.0	10.3	2.75	1.9

Source: The data before transformation for Tables 3.2-3.7 is from The World Bank's *World Development Indicator 2002 CD Rom*. All values except when otherwise stated, are a-ten-year arithmetic mean. Unavailable values are denoted by **x**. The following indicators are considered: GDP growth (annual %); GDP per capita (PC) growth (annual %); Military spending (% of central government expenditure); Imports (Imp) of goods and services (% of GDP); exports (Exp) of goods and services (% of GDP); total debt service (% of exports of goods and services); population (pop) growth (annual %); foreign direct investment (FDI) net inflows (% of GDP); total unemployment (unemp), as a percentage of the total labor force; and Inflation (inf), consumer prices (annual %); a, b: 1960-64 estimates are not available; e: 1960 estimate is unavailable; b,1970/1 estimates are unavailable.

Table 3.3

*Economic indicators, **Sierra Leone**, 1960s-1990s*

Year	GDP (pc)	Military Sp	Imp	Ex	Debt Svc	pop	FDI	unemp	Inf
1960s	2.07	x	34	34		1.7	X	x	3.8[g]
1970s	0.70	x	40	30	20	2.0	1.5	x	10.8
1980s	-0.23	8.1[f]	23	16	20	2.0	-1.3	x	63.0
1990s	-6.25	21.1	25	20	35	2.3	0.4	x	45.9

f: 1989 Military estimate; g: 1960 estimate is missing.

Table 3.4
*Economic indicators, **Democratic Republic of Congo** (Zaire), 1960s-1990s*

Year	GDP (pc)	Military Sp	Imp	Ex	Debt Svc	pop	FDI	unemp	Infla
1960s	0.80	x	21.6	20	x	2.8	X	x	24.2[l]
1970s	-2.43	x	15.9	12	9	2.7	0.3	x	40.3
1980s	-1.35	x	22.2	21	20	3.2	-0.1	x	57.0
1990s	-8.17[h]	20.8[i]	20.9	23[j]	4	3.3	0.01	x	x

h:1999 estimate is unavailable; i:1992-1993 Military estimates; j, k: 1998/9 estimates are unavailable; l :1960 missing.

Table 3.5
*Economic indicators, **Republic of Congo**, 1960s-1990s*

Year	GDP (pc)	Military Sp	Imp	Ex	Debt Svc	pop	FDI	unemp	Infla
1960s	1.46[m]	x	62	30	x	2.4	x	x	x
1970s	2.60	x	57	39	9*	2.8	5.6	x	x
1980s	3.79	x	53	52	30	2.9	1.4	x	x
1990s	-3.27	9.11[n]	56	58	18	3.0	0.2	x	x

m:1960 estimate is unavailable; n: 1991 estimate is unavailable; *1978-1979 estimates.

Table 3.6
*Economic indicators, **Sudan**, 1960s-1990s*

Year	GDP (pc)	Military Sp	Imp	Ex	Debt Svc	pop	FDI	unemp	Infla
1960s	-1.13[p]	x	15	15	x	2.3	x	x	3.6[u]
1970s	1.34	x	18	13	14	2.9	0	x	15.1
1980s	-1.26	61.5[q]	18[s]	8[s]	18	2.6	.01	x	36.2
1990s	4.49	53.26[r]	17[t]	7[t]	x	2.3	.82	x	80.4

p: 1960 estimate is unavailable; q: 1989 estimate; r: 1990 estimate is unavailable; s:1988-89 estimate is unavailable; t: 1990-95 estimate is unavailable; u: 1960 estimate is unavailable.

Table 3.7

*Economic indicators, **United States**, 1960s-1990s*

Year	GDP (pc)	Military Sp	Imp	Ex	Debt Svc	pop	FDI	unemp	Infla
1960s	2.93	x	5	5	x	1.3	x	x	2.4
1970s	2.20	x	8	7	x	1.1	0.2	x	7.1
1980s	2.05	25.5[v]	10	8	x	0.9	0.8	7.3	5.6
1990s	1.82	18.46	12	11	x	1.2	1.2	5.6	3.0

v:1989 estimate.

Focus Questions

1. What are the general consequences of colonialism?
2. To what extent were the post-colonial political policies of African rulers responsible for economic collapse of African societies?
3. What policies might have fostered nationalism in the African countries prior to the 1970s?
4. Would you agree with the concept that a second-best is equally desirable? (*Hint Democracy v. Realpolitik*)? Why or why not?
5. Is Export-oriented growth superior to Import-substitution?
6. What should the least-developed countries do to catch up with the High-performance Economies?
7. To what extent was colonialism responsible for the economic failure of African societies?
8. The obvious failure of some African countries to deal with ethnic primordial differences conciliatorily and chart growth oriented policies, set them on the path of underdevelopment. Do you agree? Why or why not?

CHAPTER 4

CRISES AND UNDERDEVELOPMENT IN AFRICA

There is very little doubt that by the start of the twenty-first century, some African countries were in deep trouble. They were either emerging from decades of war over unresolved political issues of rights and economic justice which date back to the pre-colonial societies, or they were still immersed in ongoing and intermittent wars with disastrous consequences. The net results have been a high incidence of debt (with some international culpability) and poverty. There are other visible effects: economic stagnation or decline; demographic problems; inadequate education; and severe income inequality. These nations are in crises.

The last chapter dealt with issues of growth that could be seen as an ancillary to development especially in terms of poverty reduction. This relationship becomes substantive when growth leads to a commensurate increase in per capita consumption on a sustainable basis. The United Nations Conference on Trade and Development (UNCTAD) reports in 2004 that growth must be an inclusive process, because large inequalities that are linked to a sense of exclusion based on social identity threatens the development process.

Development takes on a broader outlook that could best be summed up as the well-being of a nation. Its core ingredients include levels of: industrialization; education; income and income distribution; poverty; and health. In 1982 Walter Rodney put it in the perspective of the individual and society. At the level of the individual, development implies increased skill and capacity, greater freedom, creativity, self-discipline, responsibility and material well-being. These traits are normally difficult to quantify, and with some amount of subjectivity, require value judgment, but their attainment could not be alienated from the state of society as a whole. Societal economic success is contingent on the joint capacity for dealing with the environment, understanding the laws of nature/science, using technology, and effectively organizing the factors of production.

In 1990, the United Nations Development Program (UNDP) quantified social indicators to measure societal development. This became known as the Human Development Index (HDI), which combined measures of life expectancy, educational attainment (including average years of schooling and adult literacy), and Gross National Product (GNP) per capita. The index, itself, lacks universal appeal and it was more a matter of convenience for comparing standards of living. It has, however, provided a workable yardstick of measurement of development.

More contemporaneously, countries are still classified by such indicators as life expectancy, literacy, health affordability, calorie intake, and poverty. The poorest nations of the world are classified as "Least Developed Countries" (LDCs); a classification which has evolved with less appealing connotations from "Third World", "developing", or "less developed" countries. According to the UN, LDCs show specific traits: (i) low national income (per capita GDP under $900); (ii) weak human assets (based on health, nutrition, and education); (iii) income vulnerability (export volatility, and inadequate diversification and smallness); and (iv) population less than 75 million.[55] About 67% of the declared 49 poorest countries of the world are to be found in Africa, including Sudan, Sierra Leone, and Congo Democratic Republic (CDR).

Poverty is an apparent drag on development. The most salient question, however, is a paradoxical one: Why is it that some of these African nations are so rich and, yet, so poor? Over the years, the World Bank has tried to put poverty in perspective by defining poverty on a global scale. Who is poor? According to the World Bank characterization, living on $2 or less a day is an indication of serious poverty.[56] In absolute terms, this indicator of poverty takes into consideration the inability to attain a minimum standard of living in terms of private consumption; a life below socially acceptable living conditions. In relative terms, the lowest quintiles or deciles are normally compared to the upper segments. International comparison of global poverty is made possible by using the purchasing power parity (PPP) exchange rate that corrects for differences in the cost of living between countries.

The 2004 UNCTAD, United Nations Conference on Trade and Development, report shows that there is a close relationship between the level of average private consumption per capita and the incidence of poverty, as well as the depth of poverty when there is a low level of development and mass poverty. [57]Although the incidence of poverty is totally independent of the distribution of consumption expenditure, the average level of consumption of the poor is related to the per capita consumption in the poor societies (figure 4.1). Points "A" and "B" show that the effect of economic growth on consumption for the least developed countries weakens once private consumption for the country as a whole shows about $800 per capita (1985 PPP$) for the $1 a day poverty line, and about $1400 per capita (1985 PPP$) for the $2 a day poverty line.

As a follow-up to the previous question "Who is poor?", one would obviously be tempted to ask the question which David Landes asked in 1989; "Why Are We So Rich and They So Poor?"[58] Diverse reasons have been put forward, but the multi-dimensional outlook of such reasons is largely the result of repressive and oppressive political regimes, natural disasters, and international complicity or apathy (which some might perceive as a conspiracy to keep the poor nations backward). In reality, with the exception of wars (which are man-made), the reasons are not generally exclusive of one another when put in a correct perspective. Conspiracy theory, like neocolonialism, is a tall order to substantiate for at least two reasons: (i) repressive and oppressive regimes espouse individual idiosyncrasies and need no conspiracy to alienate their subjects (they have thrived because of international apathy rather than conspiracy); and (ii) experience has now shown that correct policies could set a country on the path to development.

Political regimes that have failed and lack any trait of benevolence have adverse consequences. First, it is easy to find political, human and sociocultural deprivations that make subjects powerless and doomed to poverty; and second, it should not also be surprising that adverse or erroneous economic policies are perpetuated to the detriment of national well-being. Generally, bad policies result in: inadequate access to employment opportunities; low levels of human capital; lack of political participation; and alienation of rural areas.

Figure 4.1
Relationship Between Average Private Consumption Per Capita and average Private Consumption of The Poor

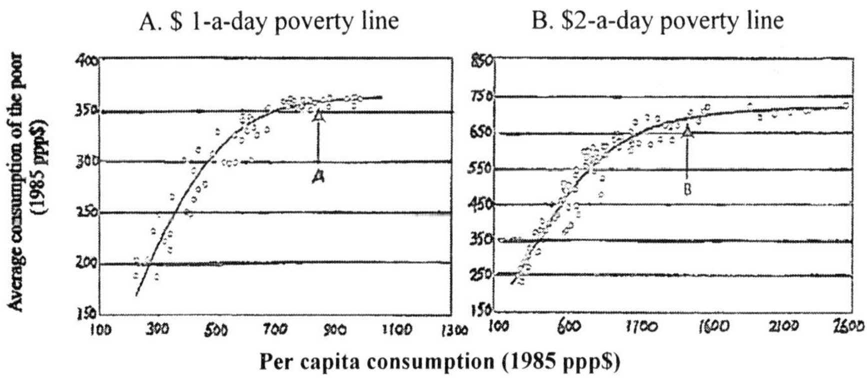

Source: UNCTAD (2002: 49, chart 9)

Illegitimate and fraudulent regimes normally perpetuate vicious poverty through corruption, nepotism, grafting, and coercion. When they are treated, otherwise by tacit approval or accommodation, there is some amount of complicity with ruinous policies. The loud argument for debt cancellation has been made against this background. The interaction of international law and economics, however makes the issue of odiousness more complicated than it might seem. This issue will be dealt with in the next chapter.

Unfortunately, it was not until 2003 that the UN crafted a resolution to deal pointedly with global corruption. In December 2003, more than 120 governments met in the Mexican city of Mérida for a signing conference for the first legally binding international agreement to fight corruption. By so doing, the world took a concerted effort to deal with the problem of unjust and ineffective governance; the social cankerworm that has been consuming most African nations for over a generation. Governments that are corrupt through and through would use grants and loans for purposes other than the desired motive and exacerbate a debt burden.

In 2002 Boyce and Ndikumana pointed out that instead of financing domestic investment or consumption, a substantial amount of money after being borrowed and arrogated by the African political élites was channeled abroad in the form of capital flight. Their estimates of flight capital from thirty Sub-Saharan African countries, which, in the absence of corruption would mirror diversification, suggest that from 1970-1996, $187 billion left the region. When interest earnings are included, the stock of flight capital amounted to $274 billion (145 percent of the total debt of the sampled countries in 1996).

The implication here is that the region was a net creditor to the rest of the world since external assets (stock of capital flight) exceeded external liabilities (stock of external debt). Much more revealing is that the assets were in *private hands but not the liabilities*.

Boyce and Ndikumana concluded in equally revealing terms that external borrowing was the single most important determinant of both the timing and magnitude of capital flight from the region; roughly 80 cents on every dollar borrowed by the countries amounted to flight capital. Mechanisms that aided flight capital included the embezzlement of borrowed funds, the kickbacks on government contracts, the trade misinvoicing, the misappropriation of revenues from state-owned enterprises, and the smuggling of natural resources.

Debt and Underdevelopment

Creditors who were once overindulgent caught up with the issue of debt and poverty a little bit earlier than the UN did with corruption, and they scrambled to deal with the issue of poverty and debt repayment (at least to put a human face on the conundrum). Tying loans to poverty reduction through the Poverty Reduction Strategy Paper (PRSP) in the 1990s, for better or worse, linked the provision of loan to some form of national prerequisite, which supposedly should be helpful to a nation and the poor. The reality is not so gratuitous to the effort —with the indebted nations still wallowing in poverty.

It took a debt crisis in the 1980s for creditors to zero in on debtor profligacy and corruption; and almost two decades later, for creditors to tie loans with economic performance and poverty reduction, and slightly over two decades for the UN to take a concerted stand against corruption. It has become obvious that debt is a burden on the poor countries not only for the much more traditional debt overhang issue which discourages investment, but the inability of corrupt and profligate governments to repay principal and interests on loans while keeping up with social programs. Why?

The conditions (political and economic) that made the countries indebted remained largely unchanged, and debts have to be repaid because they are not gifts. All serious creditors have preconditions for disbursement of loans. In normal life, creditors will look at: (i) character (ethical quality of the applicant); (ii) capacity (the ability to pay bills); (iii) capital (creditworthiness, adequacy of a prospective debtor's equity relative to existing liabilities); (iv) collateral (the sufficiency of assets to secure a debt); and (v) conditions (the economic temper of the times, the economic conditions as they relate to the business cycle). These are the much more familiar five "Cs" of credit analysis which are used as a precautionary benchmark for the issue of loans.

National debts are largely considered to be sovereign (binding on future generations), and take on conditions of their own. Multilateral debts generally impose "conditionalities" which manifest themselves in structural adjustment programs (SAPs). The initial International Monetary Fund (IMF) approach (sometimes referred to as the "irreducible core") involved devaluation, and fiscal and monetary restraint. This was closely tied to salvaging the fixed exchange rate system to correct balance of payments, disequilibrium. The usual approach involved: (i) the devaluation of overvalued currencies (to make exports more attractive and imports comparatively expensive); and (ii) to tighten fiscal and monetary policies to align aggregate demand with prospective output and available external financing (demand restraint); this initial policy proved to be contractionary, and subsequently adjustments were made. For example, in the 1990s, the IMF provided loans to Argentina and Brazil without devaluation of their local currencies.

The new policy incorporated sustainable external financing through "reasonable" estimates of net financing flows from official and private sources with the IMF coordinating debtor-creditor interests. In 1996 Frankel and Razin explained how nations could sustain large current account balances by tilting consumption (borrowing against future earnings to tilt consumption forward over many years), smoothing consumption (intertemporal borrowing to aid consumption and prevent a crowding-out effect when export revenues fall), and augmenting consumption (the increase in consumption attributable to higher investment and higher average world marginal product of capital).

The old and new policies of the IMF have generally fallen short of fostering the required development. Some critics of the IMF have largely attributed the failure of development to the SAPs, which required the sacrifice of vital social programs to the payment of debts. Fiscal restraints require spending cuts. These include lay-offs of civil servants to trim bloated bureaucracies, privatization, and reduction in much needed social spending on education and health. The governments of Sudan, Sierra Leone, and CDR spent less than $3 per head on a yearly average between 1990 and 2000 (figure 4.2), but it is not so clear whether debt, per se, is responsible for the dismal funding of public health care. It certainly could not have improved the situation.

There were other problems. The structure of the African economies is too rigid to expand the output required to meet short-term debt obligations, and devaluation was not a guarantee that the exports of these countries would increase to correct trade imbalance. A lot depended on prices and the absorptive capacity of foreign nations; some of which already had restrictive policies.

The critics of the IMF have generally focused on curative policies—if there are any to be found in adverse conditions— with less intensity on the causes of the imbalance that provoked the crisis to begin with. IMF funds are of short-term availability. The impoverished countries don't have the capacity to meet that requirement under any kind of circumstances in the short-run. The irony is that a majority of these countries, rather than being naturally poor, have been impoverished by brutal dictators and their associates. Politicians and creditors must now share residual resources. The poor would hardly stand a chance of prosperity under such circumstances.

In September 1996, the IMF, and the World Bank launched the Highly Indebted Poor Countries (HIPCs) Initiative to deal with the issue of debt owed to multilateral official creditors by the poor countries. Three years later (1999), the Initiative was enhanced. The aim of the Initiative is to provide assistance to eligible countries following good economic policies that will reduce debts to sustainable levels. Sustainability is intended to enable a country to meet its current and future debt service obligations in full without recourse to further debt relief, rescheduling or accumulating of arrears that will compromise growth. By 2001, Sierra Leone, the Republic of Congo, CDR, and the Sudan were on the list of countries characterized as highly indebted and poor.[59]

The architects of the HIPC Initiative viewed it with great optimism for manageable debt and poverty reduction, but, at its inception, there were lingering doubts about its efficacy in other circles. One prominent controversy over the initiative has been the size of an unsustainable debt. When is a debt too large to be sustainable?

Three measures have generally been used to determine sustainability: (i) debt-to-export (DE) ratio, (ii) debt-to-GDP (DG) ratio, and debt-to-tax receipts (DT) ratio. The original debt-to-export benchmark was set at 200%, but it was reduced to 150% after the Koln agreement. The debt-to-tax-receipts ratio was also reduced from 280% to 250%; however, contingent on whether or not the export-to-GDP (EG) ratio is above 30%, and the tax receipts-to-GDP (TG) ratio is above 15%. Of the three measures, the DE and DG ratios are normally given more serious consideration.

Countries with present value of debt service to GDP ratio in excess of 80% were considered problematic and in need of debt management. For CDR this ratio increased from 86% in 1985 to 153% in 2002 (table 4.1); Sierra Leone experienced an increase from 83 % to 185 %; and the Sudan from 72 % to 121 %

Figure 4.2

Per Capita annual Public Health Expenditure in Asian and African LDCs, 1990-2000 ($, annual average)

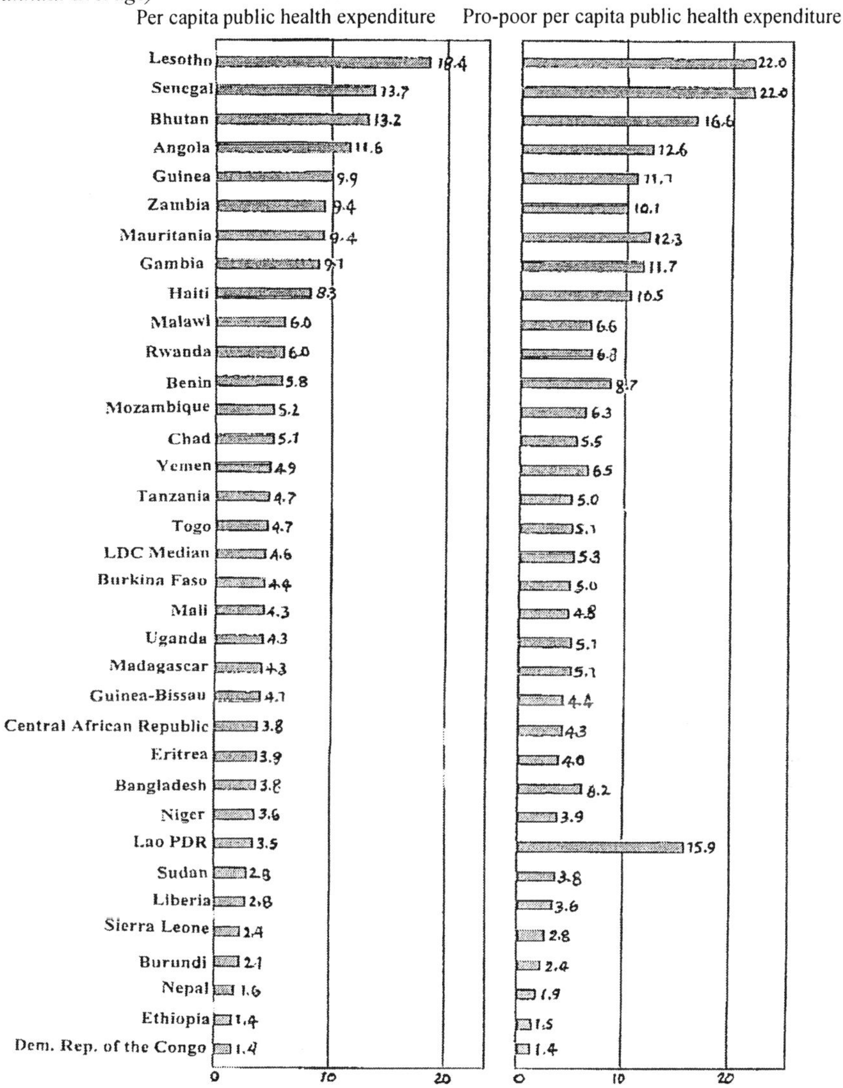

Source: UNCTAD secretariat estimates based on World Bank, *World Development Indicators 2003*.

Notes: LDC median refers to the countries listed in the Chart. Other developing countries refers to the 78 low-and middle-income countries (World Bank definition) excluding the LDCs and high-income oil-exporting countries.

a Pro-poor public health expenditure assumes that all spending goes to the poor.

with some amount of volatility in the same period. The size of the debts of these countries and their debt service obligations are given in table 4.1. Apart from 1985, the Sudan has a fairly high debt to GDP ratio thereafter, although its debt service to export ratio progressively declined. A few other poor countries show a decline in debt servicing, although the debt-to-GDP ratios are fairly high.

The HIPC Initiative is carried out in phases. At the end of a first phase/stage, a country reaches a decision point after a three-year track record of good performance based on its performance and compliance with IMF and World Bank adjusted programs. A debt sustainability analysis is undertaken during this period to ascertain eligibility for further debt relief. If the first stage is successful, an indebted country must go through a second phase of another three years, during which it is provided more relief based on good track record akin with the conditions of the first phase. It obtains relief through rescheduling of about 80% of the present value of Paris Club debt. The end of the second phase is the completion point, at the end of which Paris Club creditors provide a stock-of-debt operation of about 80% reduction in net present value (NPV) terms. Multilateral institutions must also provide funds in NPV terms to bring debt to a sustainable level through the HIPC Trust Fund.

The HIPC Initiative has faced a barrage of criticisms for reasons that are obvious. Poverty has not been alleviated, and debts could not generally be sustainable. In 2000 Cohen analyzes the problem of debt repayment in terms of the "market value" versus the NPV of debt, suggesting that the appropriate "market value" is one that takes account of the risk of non-payment: arrears, rescheduling and constrained refinancing of various sorts. The problem of adequate debt reduction is otherwise seen in terms of a deliberate attempt to massage the debt down to acceptable levels where they would be deemed sustainable. By the late 1990s, the IMF and the World Bank were conceding to some problems with the initiative. For example, Stiglitz called the Structural Adjustment Program (SAP) associated with the Initiative "misguided." In 2001 some writers like Mutume, out of the IMF-World Bank beltway, questioned the requirements for sustainability vis-à-vis ongoing obligations of key social infrastructural spending, and the optimistic forecast of lenders against falling prices for agrobased economies. At the end of the twentieth century, forty-eight of the poorest countries accounted for less than 0.4 percent of global exports.[60]

Equity has become a burning issue in debt repayment. It is generally evident that the poorer the country, the more likely it is that debt repayments are being extracted directly from people who neither contracted the loans nor received any of the money. Part of the opportunity cost involves social programs like health and education, which must be sacrificed. The visible effects of deprivation are normally seen in terms of riots, which are normally dubbed "IMF riots," as the poor and unemployed become emboldened to challenge the coercive machines of their governments. These riots occurred in Sierra Leone in 1981 and 1987, Sudan in 1982 and 1987; and extensively in the Latin American countries of Bolivia, Chile, Ecuador, and Brazil in the 1980s and 1990s in response to the hardship bequeathed by the SAPs. The sacrifice of poor programs has repercussions.

Adult illiteracy is generally high in the poor countries. The net effect of this is inadequate investment in human capital to meet the challenges of development or hi-tech production. It should be recalled that investment in skilled labor was a key component of Singapore's prosperity. Although GDP per capita in PPP terms has slightly increased in some of the poor countries, with very few exceptions, the percentage of adult illiteracy is still high; with widespread disparity between male and female education in the African countries (table 4.2). Although about 51% of men could read and write in Sierra Leone, only about 23% of women could do the same. Similar disparities are to be found in the Sudan and CDR. Debt reduces the opportunity to learn, and cultural practices perpetuate the inequality. Although the enrolment in primary education is fairly high for the period 1997-2001, enrolment rapidly tapers to a minuscule amount at the tertiary level.

Prior to the 1960s, the colonial government largely subsidized primary education. This involved virtually costless tuition, and the provision of books and writing equipments in Sierra Leone. By the 1970s, there was an upsurge in the cost of education despite the government's ambition or rhetoric to make education free at the primary level. As schools are forced to charge fees, fewer and fewer people would find education to be affordable; thereby, causing it to be an entitlement or privilege. Some schools in Africa, for the want of attention, are poorly equipped with students who are inadequately fed in preparation for whatever education they could get. Teachers are woefully paid; if and when they get paid, and are confronted with a serious challenge of making learning exciting. Education becomes a casualty of the debt crisis.

Debt impinges on development in other important ways. Sachs wrote in 1984 and 1989 that debt discourages domestic investment. This argument is traditionally known in economic literature as a "debt overhang." This is a situation in which having very large debts discourages investment, because debt acts as a tax on the returns to investment. A two-period model has been used to put the argument in perspective.

The debtor government maximizes utility in two periods, $U(c_1, c_2)$, where utility in the second period is discounted, $U(c_1, c_2) = u(c_1) + \rho u(c_2)$. The country enters the first period with an existing stock of debt (D_o) which necessitates a contractual payment obligation of D_o during the second period. Debt service payment is not due in the first period, but actual payments *(R)* to original creditors are made in the second, where $R< D_o$. In the second period however, actual and debt servicing payments are made to the original and new creditors through negotiations, but the government cannot agree to pay more than a fraction of its income in the second period, $0 < \delta< 1$. Assuming this constraint becomes binding all creditors have equal exposure (no seniority).

Debtor governments that are social planners make investment and borrowing decisions during the first period subject to the following constraints:

$$c_1 = f(k_o) + D_1 - I_1, \qquad (1)$$

$$c_2 = f(k_o + I_1) - (1+r^*) D_1 - R; \qquad (2)$$

where k_o is the initial capital stock at the beginning of period 1, I_1, is initial investment, D_1 is new borrowing in the first period and r* is the world risk-free interest rate. New loans will be available on the condition that

$$(1+r^*) D_1 < f(k_o + I_1) - R. \qquad (3)$$

An increase in *R* reduces second period consumption and the inequality (3) suggests that a critical value (R*) must be less than *R* for the inequality to hold. If *R* = *Do*>R*, in the absence of a write-down of initial debt, the total debt service due to original creditors in the second period will be greater than debtors are willing to pay, and new creditors will be reluctant to offer credit. The prior constraints (1 and 2) now become:

$$c_1 = f(k_o) + D_1 - I_1, \qquad (4)$$

$$c_2 = (1-\delta) f(k_o + I_1). \qquad (5)$$

The credit rationed regime shows that the debtor government's only choice is over the level of first period investment. Investment increases when contractual debt is reduced.[61]

Did the IMF sow the seeds of destruction? Apart from the exacerbation of poverty levels, neo-colonialist theories look at IMF recommended privatization as the informal procedure of mortgaging the assets of the indebted countries in the South to the North; which is really an antecedent to the debt crisis. In their defense of the IMF in 1999, Musa and Savastano make the case for IMF flexibility (in quantitative terms) and sensitivity to the needs of the poor in keeping with the Articles I and V of the Articles of Agreement of the Fund, which impose "adequate safeguards" for temporary use of the resources of the Fund without "resorting to measures" which are destructive to national or international prosperity.

To accommodate the severity of the problems faced by the poor and often highly indebted countries in the 1980s, the IMF created longer-term and more concessional financing arrangements. The Structural Adjustment Facility (SAF) and the Enhanced Structural Adjustment Facility (ESAF), established in 1986 and 1987 respectively, "were designed to help these countries undertake extensive reforms of their economies as well as macroeconomic adjustment."

The goal of the ESAF was to sustain economic growth and improve the living standards of the poor countries, with the effect that average real per capita growth turned out to be modestly positive in the early 1990s compared to negative growth in the 1980s. The IMF staff studies of the late 1990s explain slow progress in terms of ineffective budget constraints and management accountability. The lack of management accountability in some cases is really a euphemism for corruption.

Table 4.1

DEBT AND DEBT SERVICE RATIOS (Percentage)

Country	Debt/GDP						Debt service /exports[a]					
	1985	1990	1999	2000	2001	2002	1985	1990	1999	2000	2001	2002
Afghanistan	..	..	..	..	..	..	..	..	..	..	..	..
Angola	..	84	169	106	98	90	.	8	27	21	22	10
Bangladesh	31	41	36	33	32	36	19	26	9	9	7	7
Benin	82	70	71	71	71	68	13	8	10	11	8	11
Bhutan	5	29	41	42	50	64	..	5	5	5	4	5
Burkina Faso	32	27	56	54	54	51	10	7		15	12	18
Burundi	40	80	158	163	155	168	20	43	46	38	48	59
Cambodia	..	166	73	73	73	73	..	..	2	2	1	1
Cape Verde	..	40	56	62	66	67	10	5	9	7	6	8
C. African Rep.	40	47	86	90	85	102	14	13	..	.	..	..
Chad	21	30	74	80	66	64	17	4	..	..	..	..
Comoros	117	71	102	113	110	106	9	2	..	..	..	..
D.Rep.of Congo	86	110	255	241	222	153	..	..	..	..	..	..
Djibouti	42	49	51	47	46	56	..	..	..	..	..	..
Eq. Guinea	166	183	31	18	14	12	..	12	..	..	..	..
Eritrea	..	..	35	49	58	82	..		4	3	4	5
Ethopia	78	100	85	84	88	108	25	39	16	13	18	10
Gambia	109	116	108	115	125	161	10	22				
Guinea	..	88	102	102	107	106	..	20	16	20	12	14
Guinea-Bissau	221	284	416	373	334	344	52	31	..	..		
Haiti	37	32	29	30	33	36	11	11	..	..	..	.
Kiribati	..	..	..	..	..	..	..	..	..	..	..	..
Lao PDR	26	204	174	146	142	159	9	9	8	8	9	..
Lesotho	60	64	75	78	77	89	7	4	10	11	12	12
Liberia	133	481	470	375	405	414	9		4	1	1	1
Madagascar	89	120	128	121	92	103	42	45	17	10	5	10
Malawi	90	83	152	159	154	153	40	29	13	12	8	8
Maldives	65	36	37	33	38	43	11	5	4	4	5	4
Mali	111	102	124	123	111	83	17	12	13	12	8	7
Mauritania	213	207	265	265	239	238	25	30	..	..	..	..
Mozambique	64	189	175	191	130	128	34	26	16	11	8	6
Myanmar	..	..	..	..	..	..	58	18	5	4	3	..
Nepal	23	45	59	51	49	53	7	..	..	..	..	9
Niger	83	70	83	94	82	83	34	17	..	..	..	..
Rwanda	21	28	67	70	75	83	10	14	26	24	10	15
Samoa	89	82	83	83	84	90	15	6	5	7	..	..
Sao Tome	120	261	681	678	666	664	29	34	26	25	23	32
Senegal	99	66	79	78	76	78	21	20	14	14	12	13
Sierra Leone	83	184	194	193	173	185	15	10	..	..	..	..
Solomon Is.	41	57	52	53	55	75	5	12	5	7		..
Somalia	187	258	..	..	..	..	16	..	..	..	..	..
Sudan	72	112	152	140	127	121	14	9	4	2	2	1
Togo	123	79	107	117	112	114	27	12	9	6	6	3
Uganda	35	60	59	60	66	71	42	81	14	8	4	7
Tanzania	..	152	93	81	72	77	40	33	18	15	10	9
Vanuatu	13	27	28	30	30	36	1	2	1	1	1	..
Yemen	..	132	83	54	53	53	..	6	5	4	5	3
Zambia	200	210	187	177	156	162	16	15	16	20	11	27
All LDCs	63	81	90	83	78	79	21	16	12	..	..	..

Source: UNCTAD secretariat calculations, based on World Bank, Global Development Finance 2003, online data.

Note: Figures for total debt cover both long-term and short-term debt as well as use of IMF credit. a: Exports of goods and services, income and workers remittances received (workers remittances include compensation of employees).

Table 4.2

INDICATORS ON EDUCATION AND LITERACY

Country	Adult literacy rate						School enrolment ratio								
	(%) 2000			(%) 2005 estimates			Primary [a] 1997-2001 [d]			Secondary [b] 1997-2001[d]			Tertiary [c] 1997-2001[d]		
	M	*F*	*T*	*M*	*F*	*T*	*M*	*F*	*T*	*M*	*F*	*T*	*M*	*F*	*T*
Afghanistan	51	21	36	..	..	..	42[e]	15[e]	29[e]	32[e]	11[e]	22[e]	..	..	1
Angola	56	29	42	..	..	..	39	35	37	19	16	18	1	1	1
Bangladesh	49	30	40	52	33	43	88	90	89	45	47	46	8	5	7
Benin	52	24	37	59	28	43	83	57	70	30	14	22	6	1	4
Bhutan	61	34	47	..	..	..	58	47	53	7[e]	2[e]	5[e]	..	..	.
Burkina Faso	34	14	24	39	18	28	42	29	36	12	8	10	..	..	..
Burundi	56	40	48	60	48	54	59	49	54	12	9	10	2	1	1
Cambodia	80	57	68	82	62	71	89	82	85	24	13	19	4	2	3
Cape Verde	84	66	74	87	71	78	100	100	100	75	77	76	..	..	..
C. African Republic	60	35	47	66	43	54	64	45	55	15[e]	6[e]	11[e]	3	1	2
Chad	52	34	43	59	43	51	70	47	58	18	5	11	2	..	1
Comoros	63	49	56	64	50	57	60	52	56	23	18	21	1	1	1
Dem. Rep. of Congo	73	50	61	78	58	68	33	32	33	24	13	18	1	.	..
Djibouti	76	54	65	80	61	70	37	28	33	23	14	19	1	1	1
Equatorial Guinea	93	74	83	94	80	87	76	68	72	43	19	31	4	2	3
Eritrea	67	45	56	72	50	60	44	38	41	33	24	28	3	..	2
Ethiopia	47	31	39	52	38	45	53	41	47	22	14	18	2	1	2
Gambia	44	30	37	50	35	42	71	66	69	44	31	37	..	..	..
Guinea	55	27	41	..	..	..	52	41	47	20	7	14	..	..	..
Guinea-Bissau	54	24	38	60	30	45	63	45	54	26	14	20	1	..	
Haiti	52	48	50	57	53	55	78	83	81	21[e]	20[e]	21[e]	..	..	..
Lao Dem. Rep.	76	53	65	79	59	69	85	78	81	44	31	38	4	2	3
Lesotho	73	94	83	76	95	86	75	82	78	30	36	33	2	3	3
Liberia	70	37	54	75	43	59	76	65	70	31	20	26	11	3	7
Madagascar	74	60	66	77	64	71	67	68	68	15	14	14	2	2	2
Malawi	75	47	61	77	52	64	97	100	98	40	31	36	..	..	..
Maldives	97	97	97	98	98	98	99	99	99	53	57	55	..	..	..
Mali	36	16	26	40	19	29	51	36	43	20	10	15	..	..	2
Mauritania	51	30	40	53	33	43	66	62	64	22	20	21	6	1	4
Mozambique	60	29	44	66	36	50	59	50	54	14	9	12	1	..	1
Myanmar	89	81	85	90	83	86	83	83	83	40	38	39	8	15	12
Nepal	59	24	42	65	30	47	77	67	72	58	43	51	7	2	5
Niger	24	9	16	27	11	19	36	24	30	8	5	6	2	1	1
Rwanda	74	60	67	78	68	73	97	97	97	14	14	14	2	1	2
Samoa	99	98	99	99	99	99	98	95	97	73	79	75	11	11	11
Senegal	47	28	37	52	33	42	66	60	63	21	14	18	4	..	.
Sierra Leone	51	23	36	..	..	..	68	63	65	29	24	26	3	1	2
Somalia	36	14	24	..	..	..	13[e]	7[e]	10[e]	10[e]	6[e]	8[e]	..	..	..
Sudan	69	46	58	..	..	..	54	45	49	31	29	30	7	7	7
Togo	72	43	57	77	50	63	100	82	91	54	24	39	6	1	4
Tuvalu	..	..	..	..	..	..	100	96	98	83	73	78	..	..	..
Uganda	78	57	67	81	63	72	100	100	100	18	12	15	4	2	3
Tanzania	84	67	75	87	73	80	46	48	47	6	5	6	1	..	1
Vanuatu	..	..	..	..	..	..	90	89	89	31	26	28	17	5	11
Yemen	68	25	46	72	33	53	84	49	67	69	25	48	3	2	2
Zambia	85	72	78	88	77	82	66	65	66	26	21	24	..	..	..

Source: UNESCO Institute for Statistics (UIS) estimates and projections, online data, and World Culture Report 2000; UNDP, *Human Development Report 2003*; UNICEF, The State of the World's Children 2004.

a: Net primary school enrolment; b: gross secondary school enrolment c: gross tertiary school enrolment; d: or latest year available; e: indicates data that refer to years or periods other than those specified in the column heading, differ from the standard definition or refer to only part of the country.

The IMF programs are not always uninterrupted. The IMF survey of 1999 reports that only one-fourth of all SAF or ESAF arrangements were completed without significant interruptions. Stop-go policies stifle growth and investment opportunities. In addition to stop-go policies of the six-phase-process of IMF supported programs (inception, blueprint, negotiation, approval, monitoring, and completion), negotiations are not always brought to conclusion in a timely manner. Mussa and Savastano observe that negotiations take place over the course of several missions and that, when there is an impasse, program decisions are put on hold.

Contrary to the rule of thumb, although country authorities tend to advocate less tightening of fiscal and monetary policies and a slower pace of structural reforms than those suggested by the staff, it is not uncommon for the IMF staff to stand in favor of easing of the policy stance or for some rebalancing of the policy mix.

The quantitative mechanism employed by the Fund is known as "financial programming," which is not a formal economic model. It could be perceived of as a simple framework which combines basic macroeconomic identities and balance sheet constraints that the staff uses to gauge the size of the adjustment required from a country experiencing balance of payments difficulties, given assumptions about prospective external financing, output, growth, inflation, and exchange rates.

Why are these nations still heavily indebted? The prudent observer would have realized by now that: (i) there had been reckless and corrupt policies in the indebted countries which resulted in the debt crisis to begin with; and (ii) that the therapy for such reckless policies has really been misguided, given the nature of the regimes and the rigid structure of their economies. In a nutshell, the well-meaning Articles of Agreement are poorly suited for the anomalies which have existed within these African countries. In glaring terms, there has been a misdiagnosis when remedial economic measures are targeted at rigid (short-run) economic structures rather than political problems, which the IMF is not suited for. The time horizon for making these rigid economies variable is indefinite; particularly with the political instability that has characterized their existence. It has been a flawed presupposition to imagine that the real problem in crisis African countries is economics. Though economic policies cannot cure political problems, getting politics right is the first step to fixing the economic malaise. Some African nations are yet to get the political preconditions for development correct.

War and Underdevelopment

With the exception of few countries in Africa, wars have become the ultimate method of resolving political and economic problems of deprivation/injustice, or international disputes involving land delineation or access to natural resources. The nature of these conflicts put wars in two broad categories: (i) international wars (involving two or more countries); and (ii) civil wars. About thirty-seven of the fifty-two (71%) states in Africa have been involved in armed conflicts since the Second World War.

It is not generally easy to identify the micro-causes of some of these wars, either because some tend to be multilayered, or because they are being fought for ostensible political or economic reasons. Some could be regarded as proxy wars, where political leaders use ethnic affiliations to exterminate other ethnic groups to reinforce their stay in power, or cause a diversion to that end, much like proxy wars financed by Cold-War superpowers of old. Alternatively, groups that have been excluded from political representation, or were granted inadequate representation, take up arms to correct economic hardship and political disequilibrium. Rwanda showed that war could be fought as retaliation for the assassination of a leader who symbolically represents the interest of a particular group. What is certain is that these wars have political and economic undertones, with serious consequences for development.

Of the two categories of wars, it would seem like civil wars constitute a greater percentage of armed conflict in Africa. More often than not, foreign support and interests fuelled these wars, which complicate the criteria for their classification. Elbadawi and Sambanis extended prior definitions of civil war in 2000 to include the following parameters: (i) in quantitative terms, they are wars which cause a threshold amount of deaths of one thousand or more; (ii) they challenge the sovereignty of an internationally recognized state; (iii) they occur within the recognized boundaries of a state; (iv) they involve the state as one of the principal combatants; (v) they include rebels with the ability to mount an organized opposition; and (vi) the combatants have prospects of cohabiting in the same political unit at the cessation of hostilities.[62]

All wars are generally detrimental for obvious reasons, but civil wars especially take a severe toll. Their proximity and general indiscretion, marked by seldom-rivaled acts of savagery and barbarism, cause substantial loss of lives or decapitation of residual labor resources where capital is scarce. Capital is randomly destroyed, and the very poor nations which embark on the senseless enterprise of civil war scare off the much-needed Foreign Direct Investment (FDI), which is essential to augment inadequate national savings. The long-term repercussion is that the repatriation of investment becomes highly unlikely or very slow in the face of evident political instability and frightened investors. Valuable, but scarce resources are extravagantly expended on the prosecution of such wars; production grinds to a halt, the world watches with the hope that the wars will end sooner rather than later; genocide occurs in quick succession and accompanying it, starvation, refugee crises, and cholera epidemic.

In the face of wars, the prospects of development are squandered. The longer the wars, the more adverse the consequences on macroeconomic stability as prices soar and output plummets. Trade is severely disrupted, the export capacity of warring nations diminishes, and the much-needed foreign investment to augment inadequate savings is discouraged. These trends seem to be explaining African adversity more than the theories of imperialism in old or new forms.

Sierra Leone: 1991-1996, 1997-2004

In theory, the prelude to war in Sierra Leone was based on the mismanagement of the economy and the illegitimacy of the one-party system of government. There was, yet, another *casus belli*; the settling of a score with the Liberian rebels. The military wing of the Economic Community of West African States (ECOWAS) Monitoring Group (ECOMOG) used Sierra Leone as a base for quelling the Liberian civil-strife, which started in the late 1980s.

By 1990, there was a formal collapse of the state structure in Liberia, and the ECOMOG was commissioned as a non-standing military force, consisting of land, sea and air components, to deal with the security problem that followed the collapse of the formal state structure in the Republic of Liberia. The force proved to be successful, but it allegedly engendered hatred from one of the then rebel leaders in Liberia, Charles Taylor, who was prevented from capturing the Liberian capital city of Monrovia. Taylor, in return, directed his anger at Sierra Leone and Sierra Leone's diamond fields to destabilize Sierra Leone and acquire resources for the payment of mercenary fighters. Using the surrogate Revolutionary United Front (RUF), headed by Foday Sankoh, a massive military onslaught was undertaken to destabilize Sierra Leone. The marriage of RUF and Taylor's National Patriotic Front (NPF) coalesced around the common hatred of the APC regime.

Siaka Stevens

Foday Sankoh

The surrogate group (RUF) is believed to have prior discontents of its own dating back to the regime of Siaka Stevens (1968-85). Stevens was notorious for his intolerance of opposition, particularly from students and academics. In the 1970s and 1980s, political opponents who agitated for political reforms or aspired to the much-coveted status of political leadership were imprisoned, lecturers were fired, and students were expelled from the University of Sierra Leone.

Some of these expelled students and fired lecturers went into exile. They were able to form alliances, gain sympathizers, and hatch and nourish a formidable opposition group with consequences which were probably unintended. It is arguable that RUF emerged as a corruption of a bourgeoning intellectual movement to obtain political change in Sierra Leone. The transformed movement formed a close alliance with Charles Taylor's NPFL with a common goal of destabilizing Sierra Leone and overthrowing the APC.

The RUF launched its first campaign into eastern Kailahun in Sierra Leone in March 1991, with Sankoh as head of a RUF military operation that included NPFL members and Burkinabe mercenaries. For the next eight years (which ultimately witnessed the invasion of Freetown in 1999), the country witnessed unrivaled savagery and mayhem untold in human history. It would take an additional two years for hostilities to cease. Children were forcefully recruited to fight, thousands of humans were decapitated, and men, women, and children, became victims of amputation for what seemed to be a crass manifestation of sadism, or a deliberate effort to forestall the conscription of civilians by the government.

The war outlasted the one-party regime of Joseph Momoh, the military regimes of Captain Strasser, and Johnny Paul Koroma, and claimed a greater part of the attention of President Tejan-Kabbah. A ceasefire obtained in 1996 between President Tejan- Kabbah and RUF, which was to establish RUF as a political party, rapidly degenerated into the renewal of hostilities.

By the mid 1990s Sierra Leone had already met some of the requirements for a "failed state." It was neither able to repel the rebels, nor capable of adequately securing the crucial diamond fields or protecting its broken borders. The legitimacy of the government to exercise full authority over its domain was in jeopardy. Morale in the military was low; as military officials on the frontline fought without pay and with obsolete weapons. Defection from the national army ultimately swelled the ranks of RUF, and the government's monopoly over the use of force was seriously challenged. Some amount of international recognition made the state a viable but less wholesome concept.

As it should be expected, the war brought with it adverse economic implications for the country. The government lost revenue as a result of its incapacity to tap its vital natural resources, like diamonds, bauxite, and iron ore for exports. It is believed that about 85 percent of diamond production in Sierra Leone during the crisis period was smuggled through Liberia by the RUF. It was not until 2000 that the UN Security Council imposed a ban on the sale of rough diamonds from Sierra Leone until an inspection and certification system was established. The mining sector contributed 35% to GDP in 1998, and employed 10% of the workforce in 1998.[63]

Apart from diamond mining, rutile and bauxite mining constitute an integral part of mining revenue. Sierra Leone, which was one of the world's leading rutile producers, had to halt the mining of rutile and bauxite, with enormous rehabilitation costs. The resultant effect on the economy was a collapse in the revenue base. During 1997 there was an 18% contraction in GDP, virtual stagnation during 1998 and a further fall of 8% in 1999. By 2000 real GDP was about 84% of GDP in 1990, and the GNP was a mere 57% of its value in 1980.[64]

There has been a significant increase in the budget deficit, bank financing, and domestic and external payment arrears. The debt of the government was estimated at $1.5 billion in 2002.[65] Servicing debt in the 1990s as a percentage of exports of goods and services, increased tremendously on average; from 19.95 in the 1980s to 34.61 in the 1990s (table 3.2). The end of hostilities is more likely to reduce this ratio. For example, the IMF projects 11.6 and 5.5 for 2004 and 2005 in terms of exports of goods and nonfactor services.

Prior to the war, the agriculture sector employed two-thirds of the population in subsistence agriculture for a largely agrobased economy which is dependent on rice, coffee, cocoa, palm kernels, and peanuts. In 1998 the agricultural sector contributed 25% to GDP which is much less than the potential 49 % in 2001.[66] The industrial sector accounted for 12% of GDP in 1998 and employed 5% of the workforce. The occurrence of war meant unemployment for these segments of the population and a disruption of food and industrial production. The net results are inflation, starvation, malnutrition, and an exacerbation of the poverty level, which was already estimated at about 68% (CIA estimate).

After the war, the price of the staple food, rice, increased by 100%; and with it the price of palm oil, which soared by over 200%, as the government is still confronted with the difficult task of protecting its broken borders. The Leone-Dollar exchange rate depreciated by about 34 % from 1998 to 2002 (Le 1563.62 to Le 2099.03), making imports more expensive after stagnant domestic production.

The social costs of wars are enormous. These costs are partly associated with the loss of lives; the provision of shelter for displaced people; providing adequate food, water, and medicine; and preventing, containing, or curing epidemic. These are costs with serious consequences for the accumulation of human capital, which in actual fact compound rather than alleviate the incidence of poverty.

At the end of the war, more than 185,000 Sierra Leoneans collectively sought asylum in Guinea, Liberia, Gambia, Nigeria, Ghana, Ivory Coast, and Mali. It is estimated that about 600,000 or more remained internally displaced at the end of the war, causing one of the most serious humanitarian and political crises facing the international community today.[67] Hostilities abroad, especially from Guineans and Liberians, foster repatriation, but most of the repatriating refugees have difficulties returning to what is left of their farms and villages. The uncertainty of a secured village environment has forced many to reside in the capital city where congestion and idleness is remarkably high. The provision of adequate food and shelter constitutes a serious post-war challenge. The war is estimated to have claimed at least 100,000 by the end of 1999.[68]

The indiscriminate destruction of infrastructure and hospitals has made it difficult to establish health facilities, or for health programs to have far-reaching effect. Congestion, malnutrition, poverty, and inadequate health officials and facilities have combined to worsen the overall health situation. In addition to the HIV/AIDS epidemic which is claiming about 3% to 7% of the population, there was an outbreak of dysentery in November 1999 caused by *Shigella flexneri*. On December 29, 1999, *Shigella dysenteriae* type 1 (Sd1) was discovered. Two more cases of Sd1 were confirmed on January 19, in Moyamba District (southern area) and Koinadugu District (northern area). Reports from December 6, 1999, to January 16, provided by the Ministry of Health give a total of 3094 cases of *shigellosis* with 132 deaths (CFR 4.27).[69] The war has made it more difficult for the government to improve health spending which is estimated on average at about $2.4 per capita (figure 4.2). Infant mortality per live birth for every 1000 ranged from 177 to194 between 1990 and 1995. The loss was much higher for children under 5 (table 4.5).

Sudan: 1963-1972, 1984- 2004

Unlike the war in Sierra Leone, the war in Sudan has been a reflection of the failure of post-colonial territorial delineation; what seems to be a fraud of integration is now a test of will and failure of compromise. It should be recalled that, prior to independence, northern and southern Sudan were ruled as two entities with some amount of sensitivity to cultural differences (chapter 3). The Sudan shows not only a complex divergence of religious belief, but one in which ethnicity has taken a center stage—the perception that ethnic or cultural differences inform the making of political and economic policies. It is therefore more difficult to substantiate the argument that basic ethnic differences are responsible for wars.

More often than not, wars that are perceived of as "ethnic" are tied to basic deprivations of fundamental rights, which alienate the human being from his claim to a human status. Examples of such deprivations include the lack of: food; water; education; the right to live; the right to have an opinion; the right to vote; and the right to freely practice a religion or positively associate with others. For more than three decades, the Sudan has been unable to reverse the adverse vestiges of colonialism and reach a political solution that will guarantee fundamental rights, known in civilized societies as "inalienable rights".

It would seem that the Africans and Arabs had resolved their post-colonial dissension in 1972 when the Khartoum government conceded to a self-governing government for the South. Two significant developments took place after 1972: (i) The discovery of oil in 1978; and (ii) The imposition of *Shari'a* rule in 1983. A bloody civil war ensued which involved the Sudan's People Liberation Movement (SPLM) and its military wing the SPLA under Dr. John Garang and the government forces of Omar Hassan al-Bashir. It has not always been obvious or clear at all times whether the war is for total southern independence, or whether it is intended to gain more autonomy for the South. In 1991 the SPLM broke into two factions with the mainstream demanding regional autonomy, and the other faction, the Southern Sudan Independence Movement (SSIM) demanding independence. In 1995, the SPLM formed an alliance with the National Democratic Alliance (NDA) of northern Sudanese rebels calling for separation of religion and state, and self-determination for the south.

If the motives or objectives of war are varied and unclear in the Sudan, it is evident that the consequences are not. The cost to the country has been tremendous underdevelopment involving considerable loss of lives (more than two million people since 1998), inordinate poverty, famine, starvation, malnutrition, refugee and health problems. Peace agreements negotiated in 1996 and 1998 have generally been short lived and ineffective.

The Sudanese government, which is one of the world's poorest governments, spent on average about 50% to 60% on its military (table 3.6) during this belligerent period. This is, on average, a percentage that is greater than what the United States government generally spends on its military. The net effect is a sacrifice of social programs, increased indebtedness, reliance on foreign sources of income, and negotiations to reschedule debt payments to the IMF. The national debt as of 2002 was estimated at about $15.8b (a debt to GDP ratio of about 122%), with approximately 92% of a population of about 38 million below the poverty line.[70] Government spending on health is also abysmally low, an average of $2.8 per capita (figure 4.2). Mortality of infants and children is fairly high although comparatively lower than other LDCs (table 4.5).

Oil exports, which account for approximately 70% of the country's export earnings, have helped the ailing economy to recover from a dismal performance in the mid 1990s. The potential to sustain recovery is however largely contingent on the cessation of hostilities. Political stability is crucial to the agrobased economy, which employs about 66% of the population in agriculture, because cotton, sesame, and groundnuts, the major cash crops, are highly dependent on climatic conditions, drought intensity, volatile world prices and labor supply. The flexibility of sources of revenue becomes highly crucial to economic prosperity.

Long-lasting war has created a refugee crisis, which is a common complement of wars in Africa. The US Committee for Refugees estimates that, as of 2003, there were about 170,000 refugees and asylum seekers in Uganda, some 90,000 in Ethiopia, 70,000 in CDR, 70,000 in Kenya, 35,000 in CAR, 20,000 in Egypt, 15,000 in Chad, 1,000 in Eritrea, and 5,000 seeking asylum in western industrialized countries.

The war has compounded drought situations to produce famines in 1988, 1992, and 1998. As many die of starvation, humanitarian relief has been diverted from its much-needed destination, and sometimes prevented from getting to its targeted destination by combatants. The most obvious effect is to create an increase in the casualties of war. An estimated 2 million people, most of whom have fled to the north from the war-torn south, are displaced internally.

It is a common occurrence to have indiscriminate destruction during these African wars. Health clinics, schools, roads and markets are destroyed, thereby creating serious health problems. Child malnutrition rate is observed to be about 40% in some areas of the south, and more than 600,000 children have died of treatable diseases. At the height of hostilities, relief efforts were made difficult as government helicopter gunships and militia-men attacked relief facilities. SPLM has been accused of atrocities of its own.

The Sudanese government has been taken to task by the US for prohibiting flights to many locations in need of humanitarian assistance, and for fueling sporadic attacks on villages. In the past the number of restricted areas has increased from 40 to 60, for which the US government admonished the Sudanese government in 2004 about creating a humanitarian crisis. It is uncertain whether the 2005 peace overtures in the Sudan will be effective—as atrocities continue. Like Sierra Leone and the Sudan, the Congo Republic has also been involved in a protracted war which now spans a decade.

Congo Republic: 1993-1995, 1997-2004

The civil war in the Congo Republic could be largely attributed to a struggle for political power which is much different than that in Sierra Leone but slightly related to the one fought in the Sudan. Like the Sudan, it involves regionalism and ethnicity, and two leaders are from different regions and ethnic backgrounds.

Conflict in the Congo republic dates back to election disputes in 1993. The leaders of the ruling party, Congolese Workers Party (PCT), voted to end the one-party system in July 1990, renounced Marxism in 1991, and scheduled free and fair elections, derisively considered to be "flee and fear" elections in some areas of Africa in the 1980s and 1990s. The results of the parliamentary elections were ultimately violently rejected by the opposition in 1993. In August 1994, a peace agreement was signed between the government and the opposition, but like most initial peace agreements associated with African conflicts, it was short lived. A civil war, which initially lasted for four months (June- October, 1997), overthrew the first democratically elected president, Pascal Lissouba. Another attempt at a peaceful resolution of conflict was made in 1999 between Denis Sassou-Nguesso (a northerner and descendant of the northern *Mbochi* tribe), who seized political power, and the rebels representing the populous *Kongo* south. In 2003, another peace agreement, which looked more promising, was signed between the Ninja rebel leader, Pastor Ntumi and the government.

The economic repercussions of the war have considerably slowed down the prospects of development, which first manifested themselves in the 1980s. Revenues from oil production enabled the government to finance development projects with GDP growth of about 6% (table 5). Economic reforms encouraged by the World Bank and IMF's approved three-year ESAF economic program in June 1996, were abruptly suspended when civil war erupted in June 1997. The slumping oil prices in 1998 coincided with the resumption of hostilities in December of 1998, which worsened the country's budget deficit. The government debt for a nation of about 3 million was estimated to be $5 billion in 2000.[71]

All wars in Africa, like most prolonged wars elsewhere, cause serious damage to infrastructure. The irony is that these African nations are poor. In the Congo, the main rail line between Pointe Noire and Brazzaville, which forms a passage way for exports and link to the capital city Brazzaville, was damaged during the war.

It is estimated in 2004, that about 70 percent of the Congolese live below the poverty line, which constitutes a 40 percent increase in the pre-1993 level. The increase in poverty accompanied the decline is life expectancy, which fell slightly from 52 years in the early 1990s to 48.6 in 2002. The damaged or moribund infrastructure has made it difficult for people in rural areas, particularly the poor, to get access to food and medicine supply.

Wars create general insecurity, hamper the flow of humanitarian assistance, and create an environment for starvation and death. As the war progressed by the turn of the twenty-first century, about two-thirds of the displaced population could not be reached by humanitarian organizations to be given the much needed food and water. Child malnutrition was recorded at about 10 to 30 percent at many of the displacement sites, while families trapped in forests survived on wild fruits and cassava roots.

Widespread civil conflict, which affected the *Bacongo* and *Makalekele* neighborhoods of Brazzaville and the town of *Nkayi* in *Bouenza*, displaced more than 200,000 civilians in the 1998 fighting. Severe food shortages resulted in displacement, starvation, and deaths of about 20,000 people as of 1999. It is estimated that about 50,000 people were internally displaced, while 25,000 sought asylum between 2000 and 2001. Repatriation is slow because of political uncertainty, and it is estimated that about 30,000 Congolese refused to be repatriated.[72]

The refugee situation in most of the African countries has been a paradox of nightmare. People who have fled their original cities for safe haven in other African countries end up in equally hostile or more violent situations in foreign countries—as homeless, starved, and destitute. In the Republic of Congo, this could be said of Angolans, and Rwandan *Hutus* who fled from their ethnic adversaries, the *Tutsis*. In Sierra Leone it was largely the Liberians before the war, and in the Sudan, Ugandans, Eritreans, and Ethiopians.

The Congo Democratic Republic: 1960-1965, 1997-2004

The initial conflicts in the CDR were largely over unresolved post-colonial issues. Much more contemporaneously, it has involved the unsettled post-colonial issues of political leadership discussed in chapter 3, land distribution involving the *Hutus* and other Zairian groups, and control over natural resources. The later conflict was intensified when *Hutu* refugees from Rwanda joined the resident Zairian *Hutus* to fight against the Banyamulenge Tutsi. In 1996, the local government ordered the Banyamulenge Tutsi to leave the land endeared to them for over 200 years. They rebelled and were later joined by other anti-government forces to form a resistance movement, Alliance of Democratic Forces for Liberation (ADFL), under Laurent Kabila. After a successful rebellion, Mobutu fled into exile, and Kabila was inaugurated as President in May 1997.

It did not take long for Kabila to order the Rwandan *Tutsis* out of the country. The army rebelled and in conjunction with other rebel units (supported by Rwandan *Hutus*), formed the Rally for Congolese Democracy (RCD). The precarious situation in the eastern part of the country is believed to have led to Rwandan occupation of eastern CDR. As the conflict progressed, and as the UN negotiated peace talks, another rebel group was formed under Jean-Pierre Bemba with the backing of Uganda. Subsequently, others were formed until, by 1999, a third of the country was controlled by rebel groups. In July 1999, Presidents Kabila and Yoweri Museveni of CDR and Uganda respectively, signed a ceasefire agreement to enable the withdrawal of foreign troops, and the deployment of an African peacekeeping force. The agreement neither obtained widespread appeal nor provided a structure for implementation. It never materialized.

UN overtures to maintain peace were less successful, and fighting for control of eastern CDR continued between Rwanda and Uganda. In January 2001, President Kabila was assassinated, and his son, Joseph, who was leader of the land forces, took over the presidency. Up till June 2004, the eastern region (*Kivu* province) of the country was less settled despite the supposed withdrawal of foreign rebel troops in 2002/3, and in March 2004, an assassination attempt was made.

The consequences of war for development in the CDR are not significantly different from those in the other warring African countries. Notwithstanding the country's vast mineral resources, the CDR government incurred severe debts; estimated to be $12.9 billion by 2000, and GDP did not show any average growth for the 1990s, but rather, it declined tremendously (table2.3).[73]

As its population grew and tripled, its economy shrunk to its 1958 level by 1994. In the late 1980s, about 89 percent of the population was below today's absolute poverty level.

The outbreak of war has caused a major decline in economic activity. The country has been divided into rebel- and government-held territories, and commerce between them has stopped. The reduction in output has led to soaring prices and reduction in consumption. To fight inflation, the government uses price control laws and regulation of foreign exchange markets. Taken together, these measures have severely damaged the ability of businesses depending on imports to continue operations. The economic state of affairs contributed to the depreciation of the currency from CDF 1.61 in 1998 to CDF346.49 in 2002. To deal with the upward pressure on the exchange rate the government resorted to printing money.

The country has witnessed a humanitarian crisis, which is largely attributable to the renewal of war in the 1990s. Apart from the casualties of war, more than two million people have been internally displaced. Fighting between Rwandan government troops and the *Tutsi* Congolese in South *Kivu* province caused some

50,000 people to flee. As the war intensified, so did the incidence of rape, looting, homelessness, and the recruitment of children to fight.

Families that were dislodged had a greater problem securing food and shelter in a society that already lacked enough. Some of the persecuted retreated into forests beyond the reach of humanitarian assistance. The lack of clothing made it difficult for some to obtain food in their nakedness. By 2002, at least seventeen million Congolese were in need of urgent food aid.

The war intensified health crises. Per capita annual public health expenditure for 1990-2000 was less than $2 (figure 4.2). This is an abysmally low amount for a country, in which the HIV/AIDS epidemic was on the rise. About 1.3 million people were infected by 2001; quite apart from other health issues like Ebola. Child malnutrition increased considerably, and the infant mortality rate soared by about 40 percent between 2000 and 2002 (UNICEF estimates). The UN Population Division calculates an average infant death of 120 per 1000 live births for 1990-1995, and 2000 -2005 (table 4.5). These figures are slightly lower for deaths under five years of age. Health crises in these conflicting regions are badly worsened by the destruction of health facilities, sexual battery and bartering, funding shortfall, and inadequate health personnel.

The conflicts in Sierra Leone, Sudan, and CDR, like some other conflicts in Africa, seem to have a number of issues in common. Apart from the political or distributive morass, which is ocular and generic, they all have indications of situations where rebels and other combatants are attracted to exploit mineral resources and maintain a monopoly over the extraction of such resources. The fatal attraction to these resources has invited foreign nationals to be direct or indirect/clandestine participants in wars. Examples include Liberians in Sierra Leone; Angolans in the Congo; Ugandans (the Lord's Resistance Army/LRA) in the Sudan; and Ugandans, Rwandans, Burundians, Tanzanians, Zambians, and Angolans in the CDR. Access to these resources is crucial for the sustenance of wars as they provide the conduit to finance the purchase of military equipments and food. In Sierra Leone the control over diamonds was crucial; in the Sudan, oil continues to be important; and in the CDR, diamonds, *inter alia*.

The remarkable destruction of war is manifested in the lack of health facilities, heightened poverty, inadequate food and shelter, and tremendous decapitation or loss of human lives (loss of human capital). A conservative estimate of casualties for four of the African countries which have experienced protracted wars would reveal a loss of about 5.6 million (table 4.3). The cumulative assessment of this conflicting time is tantamount to the extinction of an entire state with a population of about 5.6 million.

The prospects of recovery in the conflict-ridden African countries are largely dependent on the ability of these countries to establish political stability, and democratic or benevolent rule. It is very unlikely that political instability, ravaged infrastructure, and contagion of wars are going to attract any significant foreign investment, or pave the way for a better standard of living in the near future. The consequences of war predict a very troubled future for the poor and

Table 4.3

Casualties of War

Country	Casualties
Sierra Leone	200,000[a]
Congo Republic	100,000[b]
Sudan	2 million[c]
CDR	3.3 million[d]

a: 2000 estimate; b: 1997 estimate ; c: 2000 estimate; d: 2003 estimate.
Sources: *Wars and Genocides of the 20th Century* and *Global Issues*.

unstable countries; one that is going to increase poverty rather than alleviate it, and one for which debt would continue to weigh like an incubus or a "millstone around the necks" of Africans.

Is sustainable development an option?

The concept of sustainable development implies the use of resources to meet the developmental needs of current and future generations, i.e., the current generation must use and manage its resources in such a way that it does not compromise the needs of future generations. This shifting intertemporal concept implies that development must be taking place to begin with. Unfortunately for most of Africa, this has not been the case. Not only is this because of the inefficient use of limited resources, which might have less to do with the concept, but this is also because of the glaring inequity in the use of resources within contemporary society. The resources of Africa have been used in degrading ways that do not register indications of development but underdevelopment and depreciation of total capital stock, with wars playing a devastating role. This clearly puts a tremendous burden on current consumption, causing great peril for subsequent African generations. At the crux of the concept of sustainable development is equity. In 2001 Hanley Shogren and White in *Introduction to Environmental Economics* put it in the following perspective: (i) fairness across generations; and (ii) fairness within generations. To sustain development, an optimal time path is required, which must ensure that current and future consumption must not exceed productive capacity at present or in the future.

Three factors become integral to the concept: (i) available resources; (ii) the mechanism to transform resources into usable products on a sustained basis; and (iii) a non-diminishing consumption per capita. The first is otherwise perceived as natural capital, which involves the gift of nature, renewable and non-renewable energy, and material resources. The second factor is largely associated with technological development, the general know-how, which is vital to the use of resources in a skillful and non-wasteful manner. In a large measure, this involves physical capital and human capital that is essentially the product of education and training. The third concerns individual consumption that transcends current consumption into the future.

Economic theory provides two significant and competing views on sustainability: (i) weak sustainability; and (ii) strong sustainability, which in its diluted form argues for the nondiminution of critical natural capital. To understand weak sustainability, it will be pertinent to impose two regularity conditions or assumptions about the make up of total capital stock: (i) the components of total capital stock could be aggregated in the same units; and (ii) the components could easily be substitutable.

Hanley, Shogren, and White defines the total capital stock (*K*) as a function of physical capital (*Km*), human capital (*Kh*), *and* natural capital (*Kn*). In explicit form, total capital stock is given as:

$$K = Km + Kh + Kn.. \qquad (6)$$

Given the regularity conditions, if the natural stock of capital (*Kn*) is depleted or depreciated, as long as the depreciation is offset by a corresponding increase in *Km* and/or *Kh*, the equilibrium level of capital stock (equation 6) will remain unaltered. The alternative proposition argues for a non-declining natural capital stock, in monetary or physical terms because of the nonsubstitutability of natural capital by *Kh* and/or *Km*. The "critical" variety of the later argument calls for the preservation of critical natural capital that is essential for human survival and cannot be substituted by the other forms of capital.[74]

The management of the environment requires global or collective responsibility. It is of no lesser significance to perceive of sustainability as a global rather than a regional or continental issue. This assertion is obviously premised on the fact that ownership of the environment or critical capital is universal rather than regional; therefore, it must be managed collectively. The situation in Africa is critical for a variety of reasons that involve population (therefore consumption), and the rapid degradation of the environment largely attributable to poverty, lack of human capital, and wars.

Pollution, which in essence could be understood as degradation, could be classified into three inter-related categories: (i) air pollution; (ii) water pollution; and (iii) land pollution. The most immediate connection of population to degradation is consumption, which is the logical offshoot of population growth that exerts pressure on the environment when the technology for adequate sustenance and environmental management is lacking. Social scientists have been concerned about this relationship for a very long time. One of the more prominent social scientists, the Rev. Thomas Malthus (1766-1834), a British economist and demographer argued in *An Essay on the Principle of Population* (1798) that population has a latent capacity to outrun food supply. If unchecked, the population will increase in geometric progression, which is superior to a means of subsistence that follows arithmetic progression. The population of the world was 2 billion around 1920, 3 billion in 1960, 4 billion in 1975, 5 billion in 1987, 6 billion in 2000, projected to be about 6.8 in 2010, and 7.5 in 2020.[75] By 2002, 0.2 billion was added to the 2000 population. Although the African population growth till the twentieth century was limited primarily by high mortality rates, and the slave trade across the Atlantic and Indian Oceans, the African population is contemporaneously growing faster than that of any other continent in the world (table 4.4). It is projected that its growth rate would taper off in the near future; but assuming that to be the case, its growth rate is still comparatively higher than the other regions of the world. Ironically, the growth rates are found to be more intense in countries classified as least developed.

Table 4.4
World and Regional Population Growth Rates (five year averages, medium variant) 1950-2015 [a]

Period	World	North America	Europe	Asia	Latin Am. & Caribbean	Africa
1950/55	1.80	1.71	0.99	1.95	2.65	2.19
1955/60	1.84	1.77	0.99	1.97	2.69	2.34
1960/65	1.97	1.46	0.96	2.20	2.75	2.46
1965/70	2.04	1.10	0.68	2.41	2.57	2.60
1970/75	1.94	0.97	0.59	2.24	2.45	2.66
1975/80	1.73	1.01	0.49	1.87	2.32	2.81
1980/85	1.71	1.02	0.39	1.85	2.10	2.86
1985/90	1.72	1.02	0.44	1.85	1.90	2.78
1990/95	1.50	1.09	0.16	1.59	1.72	2.56
1995/00	1.35	1.07	0.02	1.41	1.56	2.35
2000/05	1.22	1.00	-0.09	1.25	1.41	2.20
2005/10	1.13	0.94	-0.14	1.15	1.26	2.06
2010/15	1.05	0.89	-0.18	1.04	1.11	1.94

Raw data source: United Nations World Population prospects (2003).
a: The 2002 revision of world population prospects uses six projections: low; medium; high; constant fertility; constant mortality; and zero-migration Medium variant assumes declining fecundity, but at a level above 2 children per woman in 1995-2000. Normal mortality and international migration rates are also assumed. The discrepancy between high and low variants is about 4 billion by the year 2050.

In December 2003, the population division of the Department of Economic and Social Affairs (DESA) of the United Nations released a revised estimate of population projection for the year 2300. According to the medium variant, the world population will grow to around nine billion persons in 2300. Africa's share would double from 13 percent of the world population in 2003 to 24 percent in 2300. The new, long-range projections which show a smaller future population size, a reduction of about 2-3 billion persons as was originally projected, has been primarily attributed to the decline of fertility throughout the developing world, and the expectation that future trends in the developing world would follow the experience of developed countries.

It is not so certain whether the Malthusian prognosis for population explosion (positive check) is apocalyptic, but the HIV epidemic is rapidly altering the future of Africa's demography. Life expectancy drops, fertility decreases, and the mortality rate increases as the epidemic evolves. Each day, it is estimated that about 11,000 Africans become infected by the disease and 6,000 Africans die from it. By the time symptoms of AIDS are evident it is believed that 70 percent of infected women are less likely to be pregnant. This disease has proven to be particularly virulent in Zimbabwe, Lesotho, Namibia, and South Africa. With the exception of a few African countries, the life expectancy is in the 30s and 40s (table 4.5).

Notwithstanding the somber and sobering mitigating conditions, the urgent need for food, fuel, income and conflict resolution, puts an enormous, if not unreasonable, set of demands on the African environment or critical capital. According to the UN some of the countries which moved from developing to developed status, such as South Korea, Taiwan, and Singapore, were able to bring their fertility rates down to a replacement level at the take-off point (Rostow's Third Stage of Economic Development when the forces for economic development dominate society).[76]

The Energy Information Administration (EIA) identifies deforestation as one of the most pressing environmental problems confronting almost all of the sub-Saharan African nations. The most immediate causes are really the most expected: fuel and agriculture. In an environment where alternative sources of energy or fuel are scarce, trees become the most convenient and accessible alternative. This accessibility is made more feasible when there is a tragedy of the commons (individuals lack incentive to maintain the purity or quality of these resources because of the lack of individual ownership and the absence of Coase Theorem). Apart from the individual benefit attached to such an exploit, the sale of wood, a commercialization of the enterprise is also considered a lucrative endeavor: a source of income for the rural poor.

The unfettered harvesting of wood has detrimental long-term consequences. It has been considered to be one of the prime causes of desertification; the terminology used to describe the loss of soil fertility, which compromises the sustenance of plant life. Desertification has its greatest impact on sub-Saharan Africa for yet another reason, agriculture. A significant amount of topsoil from croplands is also lost due to lack of capital and technology to undertake the necessary soil conservation measures.

Table 4.5

INDICATORS ON DEMOGRAPHY

Country	Infant mortality rate (per 1,000 live births)		Under-5 mortality rate (per 1,000 live births)		Average life expectancy at birth (years) 1990-1995			2000-2005		
	1990/95	2000/05	1990/95	2000/05	*M*	*F*	*T*	*M*	*F*	*T*
Afghanistan	167	162	292	280	42	42	42	43	43	43
Angola	158	140	274	247	38	42	40	39	41	40
Bangladesh	90	64	128	87	56	56	56	61	62	61
Benin	100	93	169	156	49	53	51	48	53	51
Bhutan	75	54	117	80	57	59	58	62	65	63
Burkina Faso	110	93	189	160	46	49	48	45	46	46
Burundi	132	107	224	188	39	41	40	40	41	41
Cambodia	91	73	134	107	54	57	56	55	59	57
Cape Verde	44	30	56	36	64	69	66	67	73	70
C. African Republic	108	100	186	173	44	50	47	38	41	40
Chad	129	115	225	201	43	46	45	44	46	45
Comoros	84	67	118	92	55	59	57	59	62	61
Dem. Rep. of Congo	120	120	213	219	42	45	43	41	43	42
Djibouti	117	102	202	177	45	49	47	45	47	46
Equatorial Guinea	118	101	205	173	46	49	48	48	50	49
Eritrea	89	73	132	106	48	52	50	51	54	53
Ethiopia	119	100	207	173	45	48	46	45	46	45
Gambia	99	81	171	134	49	53	51	53	55	54
Guinea	130	102	228	176	44	45	45	49	49	49
Guinea-Bissau	140	120	246	210	41	45	43	44	47	45
Haiti	79	63	136	112	48	52	50	49	50	50
Lao Dem. Republic	104	88	171	141	50	52	51	53	56	54
Lesotho	99	92	145	152	52	56	54	32	38	35
Liberia	191	147	276	229	38	41	39	41	42	41
Madagascar	108	91	178	147	49	51	50	53	55	54
Malawi	138	115	221	186	43	47	45	37	38	38
Maldives	57	38	76	49	64	62	63	68	67	67
Mali	131	119	203	181	47	48	47	48	49	49
Mauritania	110	97	181	156	48	51	49	51	54	52
Mozambique	137	122	238	215	42	45	43	37	40	38
Myanmar	96	83	151	128	53	58	55	55	60	57
Nepal	96	71	138	98	55	54	55	60	60	60
Niger	144	126	241	210	42	43	43	46	46	46
Rwanda	135	112	235	179	23	25	24	39	40	39
Samoa	36	26	45	32	63	70	66	67	73	70
Sao Tome	44	32	62	41	64	69	66	67	73	70
Senegal	68	61	126	112	48	53	50	51	55	53
Sierra Leone	194	177	328	307	33	36	35	33	35	34
Solomon Islands	28	21	44	30	64	66	65	68	71	69
Somalia	163	118	272	195	39	41	40	46	49	48
Sudan	93	77	157	127	52	54	53	54	57	56
Togo	88	81	147	136	52	56	54	48	51	50
Uganda	107	86	187	147	39	44	41	45	47	46
Tanzania	99	100	157	162	47	51	49	42	44	43
Vanuatu	38	29	48	35	64	67	65	67	71	69
Yemen	92	71	131	98	55	56	56	59	61	60
Zambia	106	105	182	185	42	47	44	33	32	32

Source: United Nations Population Division, World Population Prospects: 2002 Revision. Note: Data refer to medium variant projection for the period specified.

Traditional farming practices, which are both labor and land intensive, involve slash-and-burn methods for subsistence living. The National Aeronautics and Space Administration (NASA) records that fires in the savanna south of the Sahara Desert and in the tropical rainforests just north of the equator form an intense swath of biomass burning across the African continent from December through April each year. The fires produce large amounts of carbon monoxide, which contributes to atmospheric pollution.

It is sometimes argued that carbon dioxide is a "greenhouse" which causes "global warming;" the symptom of intense "greenhouses," (green house effect, the gradual rise in atmospheric temperature caused by gasses such as carbon dioxide, nitrous oxide and methane which trap the heat of the sun). Alternative theory questions the ability of the activities of man to adversely impinge on global weather, climate, or temperature. A corollary of the alternative theory is that in reality the atmosphere does not trap heat but that once radiation is absorbed from the earth it is transformed into kinetic energy and potential energy of the molecules. The earth obtains heat from the sun and the atmosphere, the atmosphere being larger than the sun.

The much more cogent and less controversial arguments are the ones for which science and economics would tend to agree. The destruction of plants and animals destabilize the ecosystem; as animals become deprived of the much needed plants and food, or the ability to procreate. An increase in the levels of carbon dioxide and carbon monoxide obviously cause respiratory or asphyxiating problems.

In poor communities with limited sources or supply of clean and affordable energy, there is heavy reliance on biomass (total quantity or weight of plants and animals in a particular area) and coal. More than 80 percent of Africans lack modern energy services in contradistinction to 40 percent of the global population. For example, the population served by electricity in Sierra Leone is 4 percent; Uganda, 5 percent; Malawi, 5 percent; Senegal, 30 percent; and Ghana, 30 percent.[77] The crude sources of energy are used for internal cooking, heating, and lighting which makes inmates susceptible to the exposure of suspended particulates, especially carbon monoxide causing acute respiratory infections like bronchitis, one of the leading causes of infant and child mortality in developing countries. The World Health Organization (WHO) estimates that infant mortality is in excess of 300,000-500,000 as a result of the use of this biomass (WHO, Factsheet Air Pollution). Firewood, agricultural residues, animal wastes and charcoal accounts for about 90 percent of Africa's energy supply, mostly in traditional or noncommercial forms.

Africa's elephants and rhinos are endangered as the market demand for their body parts puts an upward pressure on the supply. Animal alliance reports that between 1978 and 1988, half of the elephant population was destroyed. Rhinos numbered only in the thousands, while the mountain gorilla's population was reduced to several hundred animals. These animals are killed not only for food, but also for the lucrative amounts of income associated with their market value. Income is vital when poverty is severe. Excessive hunting of animals is notably a problem in Sudan. Widespread poaching is a problem in Senegal, Rwanda, Cameroon, and CDR.

Population upsurge has other implications for Africa, the use of limited arable land. Land is a vital resource for grazing, farming, and the construction of residences. Its insufficiency has been a source of contention and friction. The ten-year war in CDR has its origins in land disputes, and the Rwandan genocide has part of its explanations in land conflict.

Rwanda, one of Africa's most densely populated countries, tripled its population from 2.1 million in 1950 to 6.8 million in 1990. The per capita grain land availability fell to 0.03 hectares, which according to Gasana, Rwanda's Minister of Agriculture and Environment in 1990-92, led to farm fragmentation, land degradation, deforestation, and famine. The ethnic violence that ensued in the 1990s was concentrated in the areas where food supply was scarce.[78]

One of the natural outlets to reduce population concentration in the rural areas is migration, which could take one of two forms or both—migration to urban areas or international migration. It is much more common to find migration into the adjoining urban areas. In Sierra Leone, this process has been expedited by politics, and the ten-year war, which was initiated in the interior and progressively ravaged rural areas.

The UN reports that the world's urban population is currently growing at four times the rate of the rural population. In Africa, Latin America and the Caribbean, the rural population is projected to decline and the urban population to increase. The rural population in Africa is expected to decline by about 19 percent, but the urban is expected to rise by about 41 percent between 1990 and 2015 (table 4.6). For the same time period, Latin America and the Caribbean are expected to have a decline in rural population of about 34 percent, and an increase in the urban of about 14 percent (table 4.6). It should be observed, however, that the urban-rural ratio is much lower in Africa.

Africa has the highest urban growth rate of all the world regions, which not only puts added pressure on the limited resources of the governments, but it also creates increased environmental hazards linked to refuse collection, sanitation, and air and water pollution. In most of the LDCs the population without access to sanitary drinking water sources is still substantial, more so for residents of the rural areas. In the CDR only about 26 percent of the people in the rural areas have access to sanitary drinking water. In Sierra Leone there is about 46 percent access, Ethiopia has 12 percent, and Sudan, 69 percent (table 4.7). The access to sanitary facilities is comparatively generally higher in the urban areas as opposed to the rural areas (table 4.7).

Poor urban areas are prone to degradation in many ways: use of cheap and poor quality fuel; a conglomeration of poor quality automobiles; poor sewage disposal facilities; and an upsurge of slums and squatter settlements. Apart from the land and air pollution already discussed, water pollution becomes a serious problem in lowlands or coastal areas. Water pollution occurs when fresh and ocean waters become contaminated by chemical, physical, or biological materials to the extent that they are degraded for consumption and incapable of supporting of marine life adequately. Runoff from streets carries oil, rubber, metals, and other contaminants from automobiles when there are improper disposable methods. Sewage is rich in fecal coliform bacteria, nitrates, phosphorous chemicals and other bacteria. Ground water and surface water can become contaminated by pesticides, acid rain (from air pollution), garbage dumps, and fertilizers. These agents could easily pollute dams and rivers when there are improper controls, management or the absence of technology to make them nontoxic. Diarrhea is one of the consequences of unsanitary drinking water. The World Bank estimates that it claims the life of about seventeen out of a thousand people in sub-Saharan Africa, the highest rate in the world.

Invariably, most of the African nations have adopted measures to deal with pollution and the environment. In Nigeria, for example, the government has made some efforts to reduce the content of lead in petroleum. In other parts of Africa, national programs for water supply and sanitation are being carried out with some amount of flexibility involving privatization and community management. The remedial costs are generally prohibitively high. For example, the World Bank estimated the cost of exploiting new water supply to provide clean water and sanitation services to all households in sub-Saharan Africa in 1996 for a prospective ten-year period to be US$47 billion.

Table 4.6
Percentage of Rural-Urban Population in Africa and Latin America and the Caribbean 1990-2015 (medium variant)

	AFRICA		Latin America & the Caribbean	
Year	Rural	Urban	Rural	Urban
1990	68.1	31.9	28.9	71.1
1995	65.4	34.6	26.7	73.3
2000	62.9	37.1	24.5	75.5
2005	60.3	39.7	22.4	77.6
2010	57.6	42.4	20.6	79.4
2015	54.9	45.1	19.1	80.9

Raw data source: United Nations World Population prospects (2003)

Poverty and the desire for personal wealth had caused reversals of policies that were intended to protect endangered species. The perception that there will be an unwavering commitment to good management of natural capital or sustainability is normally suspect. This is so partly because some leaders have reneged on such a commitment during trying times. Unfortunately, wars do not make the commitments viable either.

Unless adequate, proper, and well supervised funding is provided, the prospects of maintaining a reasonably constant or optimal consumption are far-fetched. Poverty-stricken Africa will continue to face a serious tradeoff between

Table 4.7

INDICATORS ON NUTRITION AND SANITATION

Country	Population using improved drinking water sources (%) 2000			Population using adequate sanitation facilities (%) 2000		
	Total	Urban	Rural	Total	Urban	Rural
Afghanistan	13	19	11	12	25	8
Angola	38	34	40	44	70	30
Bangladesh	97	99	97	48	71	41
Benin	63	74	55	23	46	6
Bhutan	62	86	60	70	65	70
Burkina Faso	42	66	37	29	39	27
Burundi	78	91	77	88	68	90
Cambodia	30	54	26	17	56	10
Cape Verde	74	64	89	71	95	32
C. African Republic	70	89	57	25	38	16
Chad	27	31	26	29	81	13
Comoros	96	98	95	98	98	98
Dem. Rep. of Congo	45	89	26	21	54	6
Djibouti	100	100	100	91	99	50
Equatorial Guinea	44	45	42	53	60	46
Eritrea	46	63	42	13	66	1
Ethiopia	24	81	12	12	33	7
Gambia	62	80	53	37	41	35
Guinea	48	72	36	58	94	41
Guinea-Bissau	56	79	49	56	95	44
Haiti	46	49	45	28	50	16
Kiribati	48	82	25	48	54	44
Lao Dem. Republic	37	61	29	30	67	19
Lesotho	78	88	74	49	72	40
Liberia	..	..	..	..	..	..
Madagascar	47	85	31	42	70	30
Malawi	57	95	44	76	96	70
Maldives	100	100	100	56	100	41
Mali	65	74	61	69	93	58
Mauritania	37	34	40	33	44	19
Mozambique	57	81	41	43	68	26
Myanmar	72	89	66	64	84	57
Nepal	88	94	87	28	73	22
Niger	59	70	56	20	79	5
Rwanda	41	60	40	8	12	8
Samoa	99	95	100	99	95	100
Senegal	78	92	65	70	94	48
Sierra Leone	57	75	46	66	88	53
Solomon Islands	71	94	65	34	98	18
Sudan	75	86	69	62	87	48
Togo	54	85	38	34	69	17
Tuvalu	100	100	100	100	100	100
Uganda	52	80	47	79	93	77
Tanzania	68	90	57	90	99	86
Vanuatu	88	63	94	100	100	100
Yemen	69	74	68	38	89	21
Zambia	64	88	48	78	99	64
All LDCs	62	82	55	44	71	35

Source: FAO, Food Balance Sheets online data; WHO/UNICEF, Water Supply and Sanitation Sector Monitoring Report 1993 and 1996; WHO, The International Drinking Water Supply and Sanitation Decade: End of Decade Review (as at December 1990); Review of National Progress (various issues); and UNICEF, The State of the World' Children 2004.

contemporary consumption (immediate economic benefits), and long-term conservation or sustainable gains. This challenge will further be made arduous or surmountable depending on the political culture and structure of these states. Societies with governments which aggregate interests, respond to societal needs and manage resources efficiently, for which the citizenry has a clear understanding of civic duty are more likely to obtain the prospects of sustainability.

Focus Questions

1. What factors are responsible for African underdevelopment?
2. What policies would you use to set Africa on the path of development? Why?
3. Could the war-torn African nations have avoided debt and wars?
4. Do you think the level of development in Africa would have been different if international policies were not misguided? Why?
5. Using a poor country of your choice, show the consequences of debt and war for development. What policies would you adopt to prevent either or both of them? Why?
6. Why are some nations rich and others poor? What are some of the consequences of poverty of nations?
7. How would you make the case that some of the poor nations of Africa have been impoverished by their rulers, and to an extent, with some amount of international culpability?
8. Would you subscribe to the view that there has been irreparable damage to the environment? Though critical capital is crucial, why could weak sustainability be a more desirable policy than strong sustainability for the African nations? Would either of the two be an option for Africa at this time?
9. How can the rich and poor nations cooperate to promote sustainable development? What are the problems with common ownership of resources (tragedy of the commons)?
10. What policies should the poor nations adopt to deal with HIV/AIDS and sanitation? How should these policies be funded?

CHAPTER 5
INTERNATIONAL LAW AND AFRICAN DEBT BURDEN

Why is Sub-Saharan Africa in so much debt? On whose behalf were the debts contracted? Who should pay for the debts? These are just some of the questions now facing the poverty-stricken Africans of the twenty-first century and generations to come. In the previous chapter, it was shown that debt is an impediment to development. Since debt is such an impediment to development, how could debt payment be managed or dealt with to foster development? Is there a basis for lasting relief?

Of necessity, the poor states cannot now renounce or repudiate their debts—not only because the debts are sovereign but also because it is a foolish proposition to give it serious thought. Two issues are relevant to the thought: (i) the poor African states are not financially independent, therefore, they need sustainable funding; and (ii) they will be subjected to all kinds of retaliatory actions in their dealings with creditor countries and their friends. The thought of renunciation or repudiation of debt brings into limelight the question of legitimacy and culpability for bad or hateful debts, popularly known in the literature as "odious debts."

The doctrine of "odious debt" was popularized and given shape by Alexander Sack during the early part of the twentieth century after the conclusion of the 1898 Spanish-American War. The one-time Professor of Law in Paris was concerned about the transition of state governments and the burden they impose on new governments and states. His era was one in which colonial territories were becoming independent, and monarchies were replaced by republics, and military regimes by civilian government. There is little doubt that he was convinced that debt obligation must be met, but with the caveat that debts not created in the interests of the state must not be bound to a general rule of state obligation. When debts are not contracted in the interest of a state, they become *dettes odieuses* (odious debts). Sack was equally worried about the arbitrary repudiation of debts, for which he put a greater burden on the new government to prove that the debts were harmful to the public interests and that the creditors were cognizant of the harmful effects.

In their paper, *Advancing the Odious Debt Doctrine*, Khalfan, King and Thomas present three bases for odiousness: (i) absence of consent (the population must not have consented to the transaction in question, more likely with dictatorial regimes than democratic ones); (ii) absence of benefit in purpose and fact; and (iii) creditor must be aware of the absence of consent and benefit. They identify three types of odious debts: (i) hostile debts (debts that are actively aggressive against the interests of a population (e.g. conquest, colonization, war, suppressing secessionist attempts); (ii) war debts (debts contracted by a state in prosecuting a war, the victor is not obligated to make reparations); and (iii) Third-World debts not in the interests of the population.

States that are aggrieved have options to look up to international law for conflict resolution. It is assumed that nations, rather than use violence to resolve disputes, would first seek pacific settlement of disputes. The major actors of international relations are states. The recognition of a state is based on certain defining characteristics, which are not absolute requirements, but they are criteria for diplomatic relations. These include the following: (i) a population; (ii) a defined territory; (iii) a sovereign government with control over the population and territory through a monopoly of the use of force; and (iv) a juridical personality in the conduct of international affairs. International law deals with states for the most part rather than individuals or agents. States could represent individuals or agents, and individuals or agents could be parties to a dispute in arbitration but not before the International Court of Justice.

As a term of convenience, the concept of the state does not cease with civil wars (when the claim to authority is in dispute), boundary disputes, or when states are considered satellites under the influence of a hegemon. The defining characteristics set states apart from non-state actors in international relations, and give states the right of legal equality in the conduct of their international relations.

The Evolution of International Law

The concept of natural law, which has played such a vital role in the development of municipal law, as a matter of principle, has played a vital role in the development of international law. The concept of natural law goes back to the sixth century B.C. although a lot was said about it during the Hellenistic period. The advocates of natural law saw in it, an eternal and immutable law that regulated the animate and inanimate activities of nature. Proponents of the concept included Heraclitus, Plato, Aristotle, Zeno, and Thomas Aquinas.

Heraclitus and other early Greek philosophers (lovers of knowledge) were interested in cosmology, which, translated literarily, means the study of order. The logical extension of this translation becomes the study of world order—where cosmos is synonymous with "world."

From the seventh century B.C. to the third century B.C., Greek philosophy advanced through four important phases in their efforts to explain world order and human nature. First, the early Greek philosophers used superstition to explain natural occurrences. When that proved to be inadequate and unsatisfactory, their inquiry expanded to include reasoning and materialistic interpretations espoused by Anaximander, Anaximenes, and Heraclitus.

The third phase is generally regarded as the Socratic period, when philosophy paid great attention to ethics, knowledge and civic duty. The final stage was the Hellenistic era, when Greek philosophy focused on the individual and the requirements for happiness, which was not devoid of ethics.[79] This was the era of Zeno and stoicism, Epicurus and Epicureanism, skepticism, and cynicism. Greek philosophy had far reaching effects as it transcended several geographic frontiers and assimilated others.

The transitions developed two distinct approaches to law—one that deals with the physical laws of nature, but which has nothing to do with general human conduct or behavior, and another that embraced immutable laws of rights or human entitlements, irrespective of the historical mode of existence. The universality of the claim to such human entitlements was greatly popularized by the stoics and was later given religious affirmation by St. Thomas Aquinas.

Stoicism was a school of Greek philosophy in Athens founded by Zeno around 300 B.C. From a very modest start, it gained rapid momentum once it got into Rome (c. 144-30 B.C.). It was eventually out-paced by Christianity, but it was never considered to be an entirely exclusionary doctrine. The synthesis was feasible because the stoics saw philosophy and religion as indivisible.

Embracing monotheistic principles, the stoics believed in a universe imbued with a divine purpose, in which every human being has a share of this divine purpose exemplified by his ability to reason, plan and talk. The stoics saw humans—men, and women, slaves and free, as being spiritually identical. When taken seriously, the stoic thought put a burden on all humans to strive to discover the natural law governing the universe and to live accordingly by the law. Humans must live in harmony within themselves and with nature because God and nature are integrated. To obtain harmony, the aim of humans must be a virtuous life that produces happiness that is in accordance with natural law.

Natural law as perceived by the stoics has to be realized in positive law, since natural law is the application of the universal idea of justice. All positive laws have the intention of realizing natural law. This intention gives natural law a binding force that emanates from inborn notions of right and wrong. The essence of law, then, rests not upon the arbitrary will of a ruler or sovereign, or upon the decree of a multitude, but upon innate ideas, which Cicero described as something that has not been written, but which humans are born with and are yet to learn.[80] Cicero was of course the leading interpreter and transmitter of the stoic doctrine of natural law.

There are several reasons why the twisted passions of man cannot be left untrammeled in the legislation of his interests. If, in the promulgation of decrees or laws, the principles of justice are left entirely to the passions of man, then it would be common for vices to be legitimized. What makes the legislation of such passions or vices undesirable is the appeal to humans of things that are bad, based on the human understanding of nature, and a moral sense (conscience).

The incorporation of the stoic philosophy of natural law into Roman law aided its dissemination greatly. The Romans, who were able to carve an empire of their own, were equally willing to tolerate the legal institutions of their subjects. What Roman jurists and magistrates found as a practice of law in their dealings with subjects in other nations were laws that had very general application, which became known as the "law of nations" (*jus gentium*). Their discovery showed laws which were much more liberal and capable of being assimilated into the principles of Roman law. The principles were regarded as so simple and reasonable that they were thought to have universal appeal. The coalescence of rules created a much more robust system of laws, a global system of laws, which was enforceable throughout the Roman Empire by Roman Governors and officials. Consistent with *jus gentium,* was natural law (*jus naturale*), which is based on the ethical and metaphysical (study of truth and knowledge) conceptions of man.

The compilation of Roman law after the collapse of the western portion in 476 is largely attributed to Justinian (527-565) and the prosperity of the Byzantine Empire. The collection is believed to have started in 528, with four components, the *Code*, *Digest, Institutes,* and *Novels*, the combination of which was known as the "body of civil law" (*Corpus juris civilis*).[81]

The greatest gain of stoicism was its eventual universal appeal. Although some Greek sophists had failed to see the universal relevance of stoic philosophy and limited its application to citizens of the *polis*, Roman jurists were quicker to see that every member of human society was a subject of law and not only the Roman citizen. Man, therefore, possessed natural rights, which must be reflected in law. It was this conception of rights and law that the Romans were able to pass on to the ensuing Christian era and the age of scholastic philosophy.[82] Scholastic philosophy holds that certain philosophical truths are enduring and eternal, and absolutely relevant to all ages and civilizations. The movement formed a home for natural law when its principles were threatened by positive law.

St. Thomas Aquinas further explained natural law in terms of the will of God. The Decalogue formed a suitable framework or launching pad, based on its distinction between good and evil. He saw the justification of positive law in terms of its adherence to natural law—the conflict of which repudiates the essence of positive law. The simple reason is that such a disagreement is repugnant to the moral sense. St. Aquinas identifies at least three important transactions with *jus gentium*—marriage, procurement and ownership of property, and free trade (which could also be understood today in terms of international exchange). Can there be a body of laws that can be comprehensive enough to govern the actions of states in their conduct of international relations?

The foremost scholar to have assembled positive law and natural law for the conduct of international relations was Hugo Grotius (1583-1645), who deserves more credit for such an assembly than for being the father of natural law. Like Bodin, Grotius considered God as the ultimate source of natural law, and like many of his predecessors, Grotius witnessed war and the cruelties associated with its crass realities in the absence of legal norms. His experience with the Thirty Years' War influenced his thinking that even in war, he felt the rule of law should prevail. The natural law concept rationalized by Grotius was popularized and given widespread attention by Pufendorf.

Rommen (1897-1967) contends that natural law in the age of individualism and rationalism (of which Pufendorf was a part) differed from the traditional one because of changes that occurred as a result of an increase in rationalism and modernism.[83] Humans were more interested in solving their problems from a rational rather than religious perspective (humanism). This was the dawn of enlightenment, which was necessary for a clear knowledge and understanding of laws. Reason and not faith was to provide this enlightenment. Reason derives from itself all laws without a supreme being.

The new system of law with its focus on reason and speculation was to adapt to political and social changes. The growth of capitalism made feudalism antiquated, and the state of nature provided a basis for individualistic rather than societal rationalism, including international affairs. Hobbes, for example, rationalized conduct or ethics in terms of selfishness, from which law was to be deduced. Man is not a sociable animal, hence his denial of natural law, which is the Hobbesian law of self-preservation. Human nature is directed by passion rather than reason. What Hobbes articulated untidily, but which Pufendorf tried to clean up, was that conditions and circumstances evolved to make man a sociable being.

The fundamental distinction between Hobbes and Pufendorf enables Pufendorf to bring man back into a social setting in which natural law plays a vital role for international relations. Pufendorf, by putting his sovereign above positive law in international relations, failed to see the implicit principles of natural law in the positive, thereby making no radical departure from the position of Hobbes. Can a law of nations be established?

Although there is an apparent absence of a global legislature, there is some reliance/dependence on positive law made by states. The sociable nature of men and states necessitates the adherence to law. It is in this domain that natural law in its classic form has made a remarkable impact. In the absence of the application of positive law, other sources of law provide a framework for world order. These sources will be dealt with later but one might just wonder why classical natural law has been so resilient?

The resilience of natural law is based on natural rights—the rights of man in his capacity as a human being, rather than rights accorded him by the laws of his state. The concept of natural right was largely the product of protestant revolt against the authority of tradition, and the protestant appeal to reason and individualism. According to Walker, puritan England produced the theory of natural rights, which the Bill of Rights (1689) sought to formulate.[84]

John Locke (1632-1704), who was a pioneer of the Enlightenment in England and France, also held natural law to be superior to positive law and in *The Second Treatise on Civil Government* (c.1688), argues that man has supreme ethical principles vested in man's inalienable rights, notably the right to life, liberty and estate or private property. The duty of governments is the preservation of inalienable rights, through a social contract. Unlike Hobbes' mortal God, Locke's ruler had limited authority because for him sovereignty rests with the people who are vested with the right to annul the contract whenever there is a breach.

Locke's concept of natural rights has far reaching implications for the constitutions of states. Its widespread acceptance is normally to be found in the entrenched clauses of state constitutions. Examples include the Virginia Declaration of Rights (1776), the American Declaration of Independence (1776), French Declarations of Rights of Man and Citizenship from the period 1791-1795, and today, the American Constitution. It should be noted that these rights or self-evident truths are normally recognized with the requisite contingencies.

The inalienability of natural rights is premised on the fact that should such rights be given up, the human being ceases to claim the status of a person and becomes alienated. What then is natural law? It could best be described as a system of laws that exists independently of customary or positive law. It applies to all men—debtors and creditors, masters or servants, slaves or free and is to be explained by human reason (the capacity to think abstractly), which could solely be attributed to the intrinsic or essential nature of man based on a moral sense—the use of right reason for the maximization of human welfare. Can this law be applicable to all nations for redress or the settlement of disputes?

International law

International law refers to a system of rules that are regarded as binding on states and other agents in the conduct of their external relations or pursuit of their unitary or collective interests. These rules are normally based on reasons for the attainment of the objective good for man.

In *The Law of Nations,* Brierly describes international law succinctly as "the body of rules and principles of action that are binding upon civilized states in their relations with one another."[85] International law is normally made up of two branches, "private" and "public". Private international law normally referred to as "conflict of laws," deals with rights, duties and disputes involving individuals or organizations. Public international law on the other hand, deals with states as legal entities. It consists of rules, principles, customs and agreements of widespread practice that states accept as having the force of law even by acquiescence. In the execution of public international law, it must be noted that a state could act on behalf of its subject, as in the *Mavrommatis Palestine Concession Case*,[86] and that a state can indict a national from another state for the crime of genocide.[87]

Although the application of international law is limited through international organizations like the League of Nations (LN) and the United Nations (UN), international law has played a significant role in defining the behavior of the international society. It has defined human rights; regulated the use of land, sea, and air; provided a framework within which to conduct warfare; dealt with aggression; and kept peace through diplomatic measures. Until 2003/4, when the UN came up with the convention against corruption, very little was done in the area of odious debts. This global effort is in actual fact related to the concept of forestalling odious debts by preventing odiousness from taking place in the transactions of nations, and making sure that nations establish corruption as a crime in the law of their lands if they had not already done so. This would give corruption widespread illegitimacy as a practice within nations, thereby, recognizing it as a crime in international law based on a general practice within and among nations. The convention is yet to be ratified to give it the force of law as a treaty. In the past, some succeeding states which had problems with debts contracted by previous governments had arbitrarily repudiated debts, for example, Mexico (1867), Cuba (1898), and Poland (1919). Arbitrary repudiation of debts could cause disputes or hostilities, and although these are precedents of debt repudiation they do not generally qualify as a basis of customary international law.

The international system has no comprehensive legislative body or an executive arm to enforce legislation, as one might expect in a state. This makes enforcement difficult. Therefore, states or parties to a dispute must mutually accept the outcome of decisions in good faith once they submit disputes for resolution. The Security Council of the UN, which is the closest approximation of any executive arm of government, is occasionally rendered ineffective by the veto power of one of its permanent members, and the double veto provisions of Article 27 of the UN Charter.[88] As deficient as the Council might seem, there are several sources of resolving international disputes peacefully, and several avenues from which informed decisions on international law could be made to obtain pacific settlement of disputes: treaties; custom; arbitration; and judicial decision informed by treaties, custom, writers, general principles of law, precedents, resolutions, and equity.

International law is alive and well because law can exist only in a society, and there can be no society without a system of law to regulate the relations of its members. As Brierly points out, "[i]f then we speak of the 'law of nations', we are assuming that a 'society' of nations exists..."[89] Has international law been a helpful instrument to undo odious African debts? Not until a significant number of multilateral or bilateral treaties are made to that end.

Treaties and Odious Debt

Treaties are conventions that are binding (*pacta sunt servanda*) on contracting parties (two or more) for as long as they are members of the conventions, because nations are bound to keep promises they make. Treaties could be seen as contractual (involving exchange or concession), legislative (formulating rules), constitutional (establishing foundation for an international body), or aspirational (setting goals for an international society—for example, the renunciation of war as a means of obtaining political objectives).

Conventions generally embody settled principles of international law as well as non-established provisions of international law. Though they are not generally binding on non-contracting parties, the *Vienna Convention on The Law of Treaties* (May1969), which was ratified in January 1980, indicated that non-contracting parties are affected by provisions of treaties/conventions under rules of international law. Based on principles of international law, they are obligated to uphold a convention/treaty they have not signed or ratified, particularly in situations where other subjects of international law are affected (Article 5).[90] The *Vienna Convention* was not made to have retroactive effect, but it was a useful restatement of the prevailing principles and rules of treaty interpretation. Arbitrary abrogation of treaty does not repudiate the effects of the general rules of international law, and provisions that are not well established as international law may graduate into international law by the general acceptance of nations over time.

Treaties are normally negotiated by representatives of government and subject to ratification, which distinguishes them from oral transactions or commitments.[91] Although treaties are binding, they may die as a result of war, denunciation, or a fundamental change in circumstance, *rebus sic stantibus.*[92] This change, in circumstance, must have been unforeseen by the parties, the result of which would then constitute an essential basis for the inapplicability of the treaty.

Inasmuch as treaties provide conditions for suspension, they generally provide a "compromissory" clause—a clause that stipulates procedures and methods for the interpretation of a treaty when there is a fundamental disagreement over interpretation of aspects of the treaty. For example, Article 26 of the Statute of the International Court of Justice (ICJ) stipulates that:

> 1. The Court may from time to time form one or more chambers, composed of three or more judges as the Court may determine, for dealing with particular categories of cases; for example, labour cases and cases relating to transit and communications.
> 2. The Court may at any time form a chamber for dealing with a particular case. The number of judges to constitute such a chamber shall be determined by the Court with the approval of the parties.[93]

Can a treaty supersede custom or repudiate the sovereignty of a state? In the *SS Wimbledon Case*, the Permanent Court of International Justice (PCIJ) addressed both issues, and found that a treaty could supersede custom without necessarily violating the sovereignty of a state.[94]

In 1921, hostilities broke out between Poland and Soviet Russia. Germany, claiming to exercise its right to sovereignty and neutrality, closed the Kiel Canal in 1921 as an attempt to prevent a French chartered British vessel from carrying munitions to Poland. This was a violation of Article 380 of the Versailles Treaty (1919), which stipulates that the "Kiel Canal and its approaches shall be maintained open to the vessels of commerce and war of all nations at peace with Germany on terms of entire equality." The Treaty of Versailles had already reduced the area and population of the German Empire. Apart from other losses, Germany surrendered almost all segments of Poland that she had gained by an earlier partitioning of the state.

The UK, France, Italy, and Japan brought a contentious case before the PCIJ against Germany because of the closure of the Kiel Canal. The closure was deemed to be in contravention of the Versailles Treaty. The court held that Article 380 of the Treaty of Versailles was viable despite the German claim to neutrality under customary international law. A neutrality order issued by a state was not found to be sufficient to prevail over the provisions of a treaty. Germany was not, therefore, obligated to prohibit the Wimbledon from passage, but was expected to permit it to use the canal.

The *Wimbledon Case* sheds light on the concept of sovereignty in international law. The court declined to see how a treaty by which a state undertakes to perform or refrain from performing a particular act could be considered to be an abandonment of the right to sovereignty. The simple reason for this is that the right to enter into international engagements is an attribute or characteristic of state sovereignty. Can states enter into treaties to minimize the problem of odious debts involving state succession? Yes.

The lack of a treaty to deal with internal debt and corruption is one of the major problems that has contributed to the colossal magnitude of African debt, an international culpability that is the result of weak will, apathy, or complicity as far as states are collectively concerned. Although the international community is aware of the problem of odiousness, treaties involving state succession and odious debts have progressively succumbed to death.

Apart from the repudiation of Polish debts, which were deemed to be odious by the 1919 Treaty of Versailles (because of a deliberate policy by Germany and Prussia to colonize Poland), not much has been accomplished in the area of collective responsibility for odious debts. The issue is not well settled in international law. The Vienna Convention on the succession of states in respect to state property, archives and debts (April 1983), paid attention to the serious issues arising from inherited state debts, but it had since failed to gather enough instruments for ratification. When a successor state inherits a "state debt" (a debt which is a financial obligation inherited by another state which is consistent with international law in relation to another state, international organization or any other subject of international law), the burden of the debt must be of equitable proportion, taking into consideration the rights and interests which pass on to the successor state in relation to the magnitude of the debt (Article 37). For better or worse, heavily indebted states have, however, dealt with such debts by agreements to restructure, which is also a provision under the Article.

Twenty years after Vienna and a debt crisis, nations have revisited the issue from a different and broader treaty provision—corruption. Corruption is, in fact, the major basis for odiousness. It is an unethical issue that nations are quick to identify and denounce in theory, but slow to dispel in real life.

The Convention shows that, at least, because one hundred and ten nations are concerned and convinced that corruption jeopardizes sustainable development and damages national economies, they are determined to "prevent, detect and deter in a more effective manner international transfers of illicitly acquired assets and to strengthen international cooperation in asset recovery." Ironically, this ethical commitment and determination from rich and poor nations, with the exception of Kenya and Sri Lanka at the time of this writing, is yet to be ratified. The convention holds tremendous promise for the prevention or minimization of money laundering, and promotes repatriation of assets, and international cooperation to fight corruption, which hampers development.

Custom and Odious Debt

The language of Article 38 of the ICJ reads thus:

> 1. The Court whose function it is to decide in accordance with international law such disputes as are submitted to it, shall apply:
> a. international conventions whether general or particular, establishing rules expressly recognized by the contesting states;
> b. international custom, as evidence of a general practice accepted as law;
> c. the general principles of law recognized by civilized nations;
> d. subject to the provisions of Article 59, judicial decisions and the teachings of the most highly qualified publicists of the various nations, as subsidiary means for the determination of rules of law. (Art.38, ICJ)

This Article evidently established international custom as evidence of a general practice accepted by law for the pacific settlement of disputes. Disputes are of course the premise of hostilities, and they have existed for an immeasurable amount of time. However, it was not until the *Mavrommatis Case* of 1924, that the international court provided a definition of dispute. The dispute which established jurisdiction of the court was defined by the court as: "[A] disagreement on a point of law or fact, a conflict of legal views or of interests between two persons." Measures to resolve disputes peacefully are provided in *Article 33* of the UN Charter—negotiation, enquiry, mediation, conciliation, arbitration, judicial settlement, resort to regional agencies or arrangements, or other peaceful means of their choice.

How is custom universalized? The best explanation is based on a precedent of widespread acceptance and the use of precedents to validate subsequent claims under similar circumstances and conditions. The problem, though, is that different socio-economic conditions, historical backgrounds, and levels of development, challenge the universality of the principles of law, which claim to have their bases in custom. This dichotomy of history and economic background is the basis for the "voluntarist/participatory" argument that makes the point that customs should be a basis of law insofar as states have voluntarily participated in the custom in question. The voluntarist approach creates another problem. Not every state is expected to participate in a particular custom, and disputes are normally the result of divergent practices anyway.

The impasse suggests that the voluntarist approach causes more problems than it is capable of solving. In 1950, Manley Hudson provided the following criteria as a compromise:

> (a) concordant practice by a number of states with reference to a type of situation falling within the domain of international relations;
> (b) continuation or repetition of the practice over a considerable period of time;
> (c) conception that the practice is required by, or consistent with prevailing international law; and
> (d) general acquiescence in the practice by other States.[95]

Burns, Falk, and D'Amato, in *International Law and World Order*, observe that the criteria provide a *sufficient* but not a *necessary* condition. For example, a precedent is required for the third condition to hold, just as rules should be ex pected to meet the criteria. What happens when a rule does not meet the criteria? Is it not capable of being a basis for customary international law?[96] The challenge of international law is to show that a new or controversial rule can be a basis of customary law. Clarification of customary law is, therefore, largely contingent on case law. Four cases are particularly instructive: (1) *The Paquette Habana* and *The Lola* (1900), US Supreme Court; (2) *The S.S. Lotus Case* (France v. Turkey) 1927, PCIJ; (3) *The North Sea Continental Shelf Cases* (Germany v. Denmark), 1969, ICJ; and (4) The Asylum Case (Columbia v. Peru), 1950, ICJ.

In the *Paquette Habana Case*, the US Supreme Court held that customary international law is part of domestic law to be applied by domestic courts. The adoption of a theory by states is legitimate if domestic courts can successfully identify the existence of an international rule of custom.

The appeals that came before the US Supreme Court in the *Paquette Habana Case* were based on decrees of the District Court of the United States for the Southern District of Florida, which condemned two fishing vessels and their cargoes as a prize of war. The vessels were fishing smacks, traveling in and out of Havana, Cuba, with a Spanish flag, and owned by a Cuban Spanish subject. Until the vessels were intercepted, and seized by their captors (including their contents), the owner seemed to have no knowledge of a Spanish-American War or a blockade.[97] The vessels were brought to Key West of the Florida coast on May 30, 1898 where they were condemned to be sold by decree of the District Court.

The fundamental argument for condemnation was that the court did not find that as a matter of law, in the absence of ordinances, treaties or proclamations, fishing vessels of this class were exempted from seizure. By long usage among civilized nations, however, fishing vessels engaged in the pursuit of their business were largely exempted from capture as a prize of war. For example, in 1403 and 1406, Henry IV issued orders to his admirals and other officers concerning the safety of fishermen. The orders were pursuant to a treaty he had already made with the King of France.

Britain and France traditionally recognized the rights of fishermen to fish freely to provide for the poor while at the same time preserving the traditional source of income of fishermen. Although France temporarily suspended the practice in the late seventeenth century, Louis XVI reinstated it in 1779. France maintained a principle of fishermen neutrality during the Crimean War in 1854, and in wars with Austria (1859) and Germany (1870).

The practice of protecting fishermen and people inhabiting unfortified towns in the conduct of their occupations for subsistence and benefit of mankind was also recognized by the United States and Prussia by a 1785 treaty. The United States accepted a similar principle in dealing with Mexico, during the 1846 war. However, the practice was threatened by French and British mutual suspicions during the French revolutionary wars. The practice of allowing fishermen to go about their work undisturbed by hostilities was a matter of comity, courtesy, goodwill, or custom rather than legal decision. Justice Gray in delivering the judgment of the Supreme Court on the *Paquette Habana Case* observes that:

> International law is part of our law, and must be ascertained and administered by courts of justice of appropriate jurisdiction, as often as questions of right depending upon it are duly presented for their determination. For this purpose, where there is no treaty, and no controlling executive or legislative act or judicial decision, resort must be had to the customs and usages of civilized nations; as evidence of these, to the works of jurists and commentators who

> by years of labour, research, and experience have made themselves peculiarly well acquainted with the subjects of which they treat. Such works are resorted to by judicial tribunals, not for speculations of their authors concerning what the law ought to be, but for trustworthy evidence of what the law really is.[98]

In the *Asylum Case* (Columbia v. Peru) 1950 ICJ, the court held that state failure to ratify conventions, by open opposition does not make a "custom" binding on that state. Open opposition must be contrasted with acquiescence, which means tacit approval or the absence of clear and pointed opposition.

Burns, Falk and D'Amato suggest that to clearly understand the Hudson criteria for customary law two broad perspectives are helpful—material and psychological. The material focuses on what states actually do, and the psychological deals with the thought (conception) pattern behind state action. This distinction is necessary to prevent all state actions from being legal.[99] Case law clarifies intent. What then is customary International law?

The position of the international court on *The SS Lotus Case* provides a good summary of customary international law. The following are the salient issues: (i) rules of law binding upon states emanate from their free will; (ii) the rules come from conventions or usages that express principles of law; and (iii) principles of law are established to achieve a common objective or regulate relations between co-existing independent communities. It should be noted that common objective incorporates the concept of what is material and psychological. It, therefore, precludes arbitrary selfish objectives not supported by the general principles of law. Alternatively, customary law presupposes an obligation on a state as a member of a society—the international community.

Is debt repudiation a customary matter? Is the lack of repudiation a source of underdevelopment? The lack of widespread repudiation as accepted practice even when debts are perceptibly odious or hateful, and the established principle that sovereign debt is an obligation which is binding on a successor state or government make it difficult to justify debt repudiation on a customary basis. As a matter of fact debt rescheduling has become a principled method of mitigation rather than repudiation. Problems therefore attend the invocation of custom as a basis for debt repudiation in international law. It must be shown in principle that repudiation of odious debts is generally recognized or accepted among civilized nations, even by acquiescence, or that highly qualified publicists of various nations affirm such a practice.

One experience that might have laid the basis for a claim to repudiation was the Treaty of Versailles (1919) concerning the repudiation of Polish debt. Yet this was a treaty for which the principle of debt repudiation is yet to find general agreement in international law. The case of Great Britain v. Costa Rica, otherwise known as the Tinoco Arbitration, makes it even more difficult for successor governments to repudiate prior obligations, however odious those obligations might have been. This case will be discussed later.

It is unlikely that debt repudiation could have benefited the poor and underdeveloped African nations because of their dependence on sustainable finance to offset the problems associated with odiousness and corruption. Prospects of retaliation or denial of subsequent credit, or even the nature of debt contracts make judicial recourse or arbitration less likely. In the absence of debt repudiation and the presence of costly debt rescheduling, underdeveloped and heavily indebted African countries could hope for one of three remedies:
(i) generous and/or fair rescheduling of debts; (ii) partial debt cancellation; and (iii) total debt cancellation, a decision that has to be made based on equity, or proportionality.

The case for equity or proportionality is a compelling one. If hateful debts had been recklessly and decisively contracted by fraudulent and profligate regimes with the blessings of overindulgent creditors, then there has to be some meaningful mitigating considerations for those who must now to pay a heavy burden of the hateful debts but who derived residual benefits that make it impossible for them to justify the claim of odiousness.

Arbitration and Odious Debts

The 1899 and 1907 Hague Conventions presented clear objectives of international arbitration when there are disputes between international states or agents. Arbitration lends itself to fewer rigors than a settlement in the international court. Judges are important for both processes, but each has different procedures and impact on the development of international law.

In his *The Law of Nations,* Brierly points out that a standing court develops judicial tradition from case to case. "It is therefore not only a means of settling disputes, but to some extent a means of preventing them from arising."[100] However, in tribunals and much more formal courts, judges interpret law with very little or no discretionary power to disregard the law. They are obligated to interpret the law and not to replace the law by their opinions. When disputants opt for arbitration they are, therefore, doing so based on respect for law and by implication, a humble submission to the judgment of both courts in good faith.

Arbitration provides a much more viable settlement of disputes between states and non-state parties. Unlike the ICJ where only states could be parties to a dispute, non-state parties, especially for debts involving states and financial institutions could seek settlement by arbitration. In both courts, the decisions are binding and final.[101]

One of the most prominent cases involving sovereign debt repudiation on the basis of odiousness was the 1923 Tinoco Arbitration case decided by Chief Justice Taft. By every measure of the standards of odiousness today, the case for odiousness then was equally compelling. In 1917, Tinoco overthrew the then existing government of Costa Rica under President Alfredo Gonzalez—a typical *coup d'état* that is familiar to most African countries. Tinoco then established a new constitution that lasted till 1919 after which the old constitution was restored. In 1922, however the new government passed legislation known as the *Law of Nullities No.41*, nullifying all engagements entered into by Tinoco's government.

During the period of the illegitimate Tinoco government, the Tinoco government contracted loans with the Royal Bank of Canada to the sum of 998, 000 Costa Rican Colones (CR), and made a treaty with Great Britain, whereby the Central Costa Rica Petroleum Company was to obtain rights to explore for and exploit oil deposits in Costa Rica. British subjects held shares of the Royal Bank of Canada and the Central Costa Rica Petroleum Company. The case that went before the arbitrator concerned the legitimacy of the *Law of Nullities* and the annulment of both the debt and the prospects of exploring and exploiting oil deposits.

The Costa Rican government presented the following arguments: (i) that the Tinoco government was not a *de facto* or *de jure* government according to the rules of international law; (ii) that the contracts of the Tinoco government as they pertain to Great Britain on behalf of her subjects were void because the government of Tinoco and its acts were in violation of the 1871 Costa Rican Constitution; (iii) that the Tinoco government had dubious legitimacy during its incumbency in the eyes of Great Britain; and (iv) that the contracts of the British subjects were enforceable under Costa Rican law without diplomatic interference.

The British claims and the findings of the Chief Justice shed more light on the issue of odious debts. The British contended that: (i) the Tinoco government was the only government of Costa Rica *de facto* and *de jure* for two years and nine months, during which time there was no other government disputing its sovereignty (its people acquiesced and never had an alternative government); and (ii) that a succeeding government could not by legislative decree avoid responsibility for the acts of a preceding government by a confiscation of the property of foreign subjects except in violation of international law.

The chief Justice found that restored government could not repudiate the obligations which a prior government had imposed on a state, and that the issue must be resolved by evidence of fact rather than municipal law. Therefore, it would be immaterial if the Tinoco government was unconstitutional.

What raises an issue and concern about the odiousness of the African debts is the lack of tacit acceptance of the indebted regimes and the lack of an evident alternative government contesting sovereignty. Like the Tinoco regime, some of these African regimes enjoy international recognition. The Chief Justice, Taft, in his ruling found that apart from the US and other allies, at least twenty nations extended recognition to the Tinoco regime between April and December of 1917. Non-recognition of a government by other nations is usually an indication that the government has not attained the independence or control required to entitle it to be recognized as a government in international law. The municipal court of a country that had not recognized the Tinoco government might have ruled otherwise, but this was an international tribunal.

The legitimacy of courts enforcing the instruments of a restored authority was questioned on the basis of prejudice and full effect on international law. Other nations may clearly object to a tribunal whose decision is based on legislation enacted after the fact. The clear ruling of the Chief Justice is that the identity of a state is not affected by a change of government. A new government succeeds to the rights and obligations of its predecessor.

Is the ICJ an Avenue for Odious Debt Settlement?

Judicial decisions are judgments of courts dealing with contentious claims. As such they must not be confused with advisory opinions. They are generally designed to promote the pacific settlement of disputes. Article 38 (d) of the Statute of the ICJ alludes to the authoritative work of publicists and judicial decisions of nations as a "subsidiary means for the deter-mi-nation of rules of law."

Judicial decisions are powerful because of the precedents they establish. Such decisions are generally cited by parties to a dispute trying to legitimize their position on points of law based on what transpired in the past and the rules that were established then. The hopes of disputants are largely based on the doctrine of *stare decisis*, the expectation that rules of law which were pertinent to previous cases are relevant or appropriate to subsequent cases of similar facts.

Article 59 of the Statute of the ICJ warns against the general application of the doctrine. "The decision of the Court has no binding force except between the parties and in respect of that particular case". In actual fact, as a practical matter, rule adjudication lends itself to the weight of precedence, and the weight of precedence should not seriously be discounted. Customary international law, for example, is heavily dependent on case law, which is what municipal and international courts have accepted as law. The law of judicial decisions in international relations is, therefore, a law of municipal courts and international tribunals that owe a great deal to precedent, probably more than the Statute of the International Court would be willing to admit. For example, cases involving international disputes like *Thirty Hogsheads of Sugar v. Boyle*[102] have relied on precedent, municipal court rulings, and the accepted practice of civilized nations.

The case, which came to the US Supreme Court from the Circuit Court for the district of Maryland, condemned 30 hogsheads of Sugar as a prize of war. The 30 hogsheads of sugar belonged to a Danish subject, Adrian Bentzon, who owned a plantation in Santa Cruz prior to the capture of the Island by the British (then under Denmark) and thereafter.

After the capture of Santa Cruz, Bentzon withdrew from the Island, settled in the U.S. and Denmark; but he shipped 30 hogsheads of sugar from his plantation in Santa Cruz to a house in London as an attempt to hedge the risk of expropriation. In July, 1812, after the declaration of war by the U.S. against Great Britain, the sugar, which was en route to London in a British ship, was interdicted by officers and crew of the U.S. privateer, Comet, brought to Baltimore, and labeled as British property; hence, it was a prize of war. The following issues arose from the case: (i) Was Bentzon a neutral party (a Danish citizen who had not incorporated his interest with Britain) who was entitled to his property?; (ii) Was the case within the applicable rules established by British prize courts?; (iii) If the case was within the applicable rules established by British prize courts, were those rules to be considered municipal law in America?; (iv) If the case was within the applicable rules established by British prize courts, were those rules to be applied to a neutral nation that had never adopted them?; and (v) Did the capture of Santa Cruz immediately make Santa Cruz the property of Great Britain (i.e.) its land and products thereof ?

One of the many interesting issues of the case was the application of British municipal prize laws to a nation that had not remonstrated openly against such laws (acquiesced). Chief Justice Marshall delivered the opinion of the U.S. Supreme Court. The court relied on a prior case (precedent), which was known as the *Phoenix Case,*[103] and the general practice and laws of civilized nations.

In the *Phoenix Case,* the British captured a vessel *en route* from Surinam to Holland. Part of the cargo belonged to persons residing in Germany (a neutral country), a product of their estates in Surinam. The rule concerning acquiescence and neutrality was considered settled, and was not given much consideration. The following were integral components of the opinion:

(i) although acquisitions made during a war are not to be considered as permanent until confirmed by a treaty, yet to every commercial and belligerent purpose, they are considered as part of the domain of the conqueror, so long as he retains the possession and government of them;

(ii) transactions of the type made by Bentzon take on a national character independent of peace or war (the produce of a person's own plantation in the colony of the enemy, though shipped in time of peace, is liable to be considered as property of the enemy, because the proprietor has incorporated himself with the permanent interests of the nation as a holder of the soil);[104]

(iii) while the island belonged to Denmark, the produce of the soil, while unsold, was Danish property, whatever might be the general nationality of the proprietor (when the Island became British, the soil and its produce, while that produce remained unsold, were British);

(iv) the case was within the rule as laid down in the British Courts;

(v) the law of nations, recognized by all civilized and commercial states throughout Europe and America, is the great source from which rules respecting belligerent and neutral rights are derived (this law is in part unwritten and in part conventional);

(vi) to ascertain that which is unwritten, resort is made to the great principles of reason and justice (these principles are understood differently by different nations under different circumstances but are made to be settled by a series of judicial decisions);

(vii) the decisions of the courts of every country, so far as they are founded upon law common to every country, will be received, not as authority, but with respect (the decisions of the courts of every country show how the law of nations, in a given case, is understood in that country, and will be given consideration in adopting a rule for a prevailing case); and

(viii) the United States having, at one time formed a component part of the British Empire, adopted British prize law as American prize law.

The adaptation of British prize law continued even after independence, and was not modified by the American Congress. Yet this relationship does not supersede respect for rules of other countries.

Judicial decisions have formed a significant basis for the application of international law to ensure stability and fairness. Modern bilateral or multilateral debt arrangements/contracts have clauses like compromissory clauses which provide for dispute settlement without the ICJ. These arrangements minimize the role of the Court in developing a judicial tradition. Multilateral institutions like the IMF and World Bank have full juridical personality but are obviously not states and cannot therefore be brought in front of the Court. Without an IMF waiver, the IMF and its assets are immune from every judicial process and its assets cannot be expropriated or confiscated (Article IX (3) and (4) of its Articles of Agreement). Unlike the IMF, the World Bank could be sued (highly unlikely), but like the IMF its assets are immune from expropriation or confiscation (Article VII (3) and (4) of its Articles). In addition to other sources at the disposal of the Court, the Court applies general principles of law.

Use of General Principles of Law in Judicial Settlement

The application of the general principles of law is a safeguard for the just application of law when other sources of international law are inadequate. "Principles" are a synonym for "axioms."[105] These axioms are generally believed to have general appeal to civilized nations.[106] These principles of law, private and public are of fundamental character. Some of these axioms, which are so prevalent today, are founded in legal experience and include the following:

(i) a man cannot be a judge in his own cause;
(ii) a breach of legal duty requires the obligation of restitution;
(iii) abuse of right is repugnant in the eyes of law;
(iv) an accused is presumed innocent until proven culpable;
(v) legal obligations must be exercised in good faith;
(vi) prosecution of crimes is discretionary and not compelled; and
(vii) justice delayed is justice denied.

It is generally believed that these axioms are fundamental facilitators of fairness/justice with widespread appeal to all civilized societies.

According to Professor Janis, axioms make it difficult to advance the argument that the basis for the use of the general principles of law is vested in one of three theories: (i) the need to apply natural law as opposed to positive law; (ii) the necessity to have state consent, *opinio juris;* (iii) the general appeal, irrespective of speculative law, convention, and custom.[107]

Deep thought of the legal experience of civilized nations would realistically make the attribution of the principles to any particular theory worthless. Cheng wrote the following about principles:

> Principles are to be distinguished from rules... This part of international law does not consist... in specific rules formulated for practical purposes, but in general propositions underlying the various rules of law which express the essential qualities of juridical truth itself, in short of Law.[108]

In the *Chorzow Factory Case* of 1927, for example, the P.C.I.J. applied the general principles of law.[109]

On March 5, 1915, a contract was concluded between the Chancellor of the German Empire, on behalf of the Reich, and the Bayerische according to which the company was to establish for the Reich, amongst other things, a nitrate factory at Chorzow in Upper Silesia. Land was to be obtained for the Reich and registered in its name in the land register. The land was eventually registered in the name of the Reich. The company was to manage the factory until March 31, 1941. The Reich had the right, commencing on March 31, 1926, to terminate the contract for the management of the factory by the company on March 31 of any subsequent year within the contract upon fifteen month's notice. The company (Bayerische) was entitled to make use of all patents, licenses, experience gained, innovations and improvements, as well as all supply and delivery contracts of which it had the benefit.

On May 14, 1919, contractual problems arose between the Reich and the Bayerische Company, but the problems were eventually settled out of court on October 24, 1919. A series of new legal instruments led to the formation of a new company on December 24, 1919, known as the *Oberschlesische Stickstoffwerke* (hereinafter called OS). The Reich sold the factory at Chorzow to the new company, OS. By the purchase, OS was to possess the land, buildings and installations in addition to accessories, reserves, raw material, equipment and stocks, but the management and working of the factory remained in the hands of the Bayerische for the purpose of utilizing patents, licenses, experience, and contracts. Another company with limited liability, known as the *Stickstoff Treuhand Gesellschaft m. b. H.* (hereinafter called Treuhand) took over the debt obligations of the OS to the Reich, and obtained shares of the OS to the tune of approximately 110 million marks.[110] The OS was duly registered on January 29, 1920, as owner of the landed property constituting the nitrate factory at Chorzow. The registered office of the OS, which under the memorandum of association, was established at Chorzow, was subsequently transferred to Berlin by an amendment executed on January 14, 1920. On May 15, 1922, a treaty was signed at Geneva between Germany and Poland concerning Upper Silesia.

On July 1, 1922, the Polish Court of *Huta Krolewska* ruled that the registration of the OS as owner of the Chorzow factory was to be cancelled, i.e., declared null and void, and that the right of ownership in the landed property in question was to be registered in the name of the Polish Treasury (Judgment No.7).

On July 3, 1922, pursuant to a Polish ministerial decree of June 24, 1922, M.Ignacy Moscicki, who was delegated with full powers to take charge of the factory at Chorzow, took possession of the factory and management in accordance with the terms of the decree.

After taking over the factory, the Polish government entered it in the list of property transferred to it under Article 256 of the Treaty of Versailles. The OS brought an action before the German-Polish Mixed Arbitral Tribunal at Paris on November 15, 1922, calling for among other things, the restoration of the factory. The complaint was, however, withdrawn before a decision was given.[111] A parallel action against the Polish Treasury was brought before the Civil Court of Katowice for payment of equivalent value or restitution to the OS or the Bayerische, but no decision was made on the merits.

The German government initiated negotiations, but it became apparent by January 1927, that the restoration of the factory was impossible mainly because Poland wanted some of its claims to be set off against the indemnity to be awarded to Germany. The case was then brought to the PCIJ on February 8, 1927, by Germany.[112] Two central issues are involved which required the application of general principles of law (i) restitution; and (ii) payment for losses or indemnity. Other issues that will not be referred to in detail here included the following:

(i) was the expropriation of the factory legal;
(ii) did Germany have a choice of remedies between restitution of the property taken, *restitution in integrum*, and a claim of damages;
(iii) should there be an indemnity, if so, of what magnitude and on what basis;
(iv) was the OS the owner of the lands and buildings which were entered in its name in the land register from January 1920 till 1922 when the entry was vacated in accordance with Polish law of 1920;[113]
(v) was the contract of 1919 and the transfer of the factory to the OS fictitious and fraudulent; and
(vi) should German municipal law, which was in force in Polish Upper Silesia, take precedence over the International Court on such issues as property in Polish Upper Silesia?

The International Court was first and foremost confronted with the issue of jurisdiction, which Poland had raised. Poland contended that the Court had no jurisdiction over the case, but Germany argued that even if the arbitration clause contained in Article 23 of the Geneva Convention, did not apply, the Court would have jurisdiction under the Arbitration Treaty of Locarno. Article 23 of the Geneva Convention gives the Court jurisdiction for "differences of opinion, resulting from the interpretation of Articles 6 to 22", which may arise between the German Government and the Polish Government. The Polish government wanted to exclude reparation issues, but the Court disagreed and based its jurisdiction on paragraph 1 of Article 23.

The Court found that the dispossession of OS and Bayerische was wrongful. The Geneva Convention did not abolish the liquidation regime instituted by the Treaty of Versailles, but it limited it in several respects. For example, Articles 92 and 297 of the Geneva Convention, allowed private persons to appeal to the Mixed Arbitral Tribunal. The right to do so was given to the interested party, so that in the event of a sale or other measures taken by the liquidating government which will be prejudicial to price, a tribunal may then be able to grant reasonable indemnity.

In dealing with the case the International Court applied the following principles:

(i) it is a principle in international law that the breach of an engagement involves an obligation to make reparation in an adequate form (reparation therefore is the indispensable complement of a failure to apply a convention and there is no necessity for this to be stated in the convention);

(ii) the principle of respect for vested rights (arbitral clauses as expressed in Article 23, are intended to avert the possibility that in consequence of the existence of a persistent difference of opinion between contracting parties, interests may be compromised); and

(iii) one party (respondent) cannot avail himself of the fact that the other (complainant) has not fulfilled some obligation or has not had recourse to some means of redress, if the former party (respondent) has by some illegal act, prevented the latter (complainant) from fulfilling the obligation in question, or from having recourse to the tribunal which would have been open to him.

The dispossession took place without previous investigation of the right of ownership; the possible undertaking of this investigation in order to justify the dispossession after it has taken place cannot undo the fact that a breach of the Geneva convention has already taken place, or affect the Court's jurisdiction.

Use of Equity in Judicial Settlement

When customs, treaties, and general principles of law are inadequate, the International Court is empowered to use equity. Equity is a power that is seldom used, and it is yet another safeguard in the application of international law to dispute resolution.

Equity is simply the right to exercise judicial discretion when unforeseen contingencies have made it more convoluted to interpret the intention of treaties, the spirit of laws, or the attainment of compromise. As such, it is used to fix or correct an unintended wrong or misperception in the formation of a consensus or

Denmark, Netherlands, and West Germany

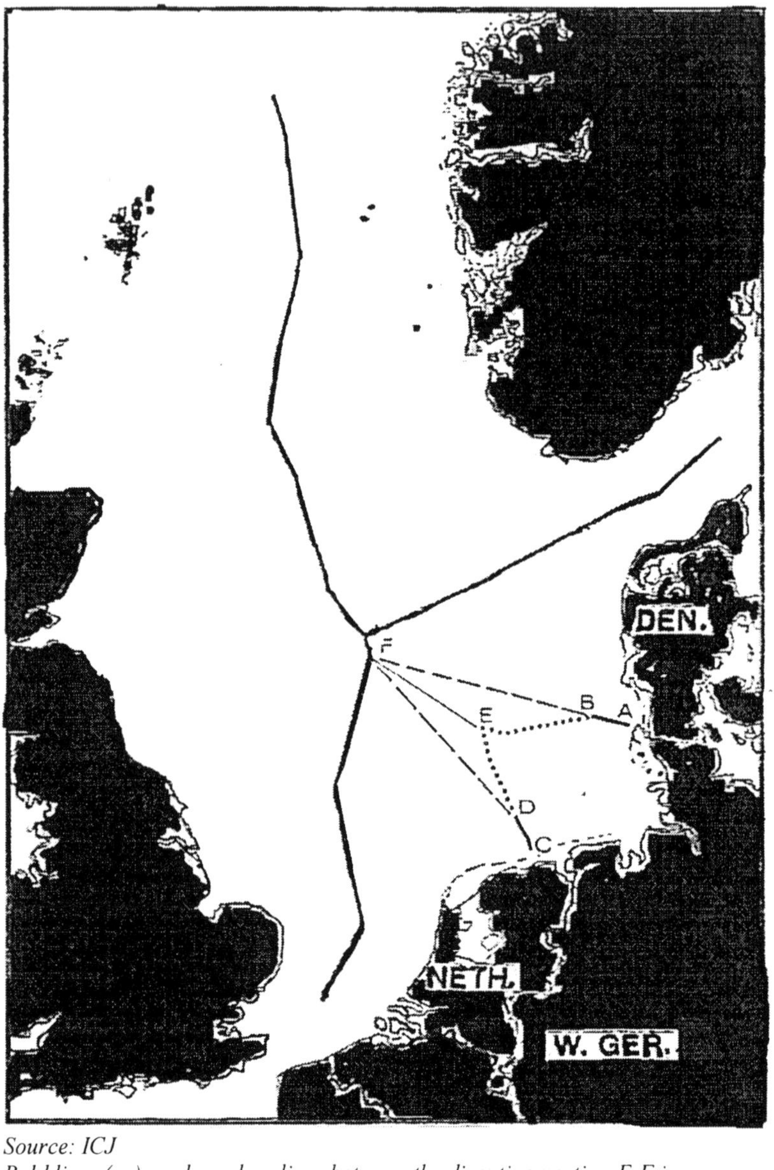

Source: ICJ
Bold lines (—) are boundary lines between the disputing parties. E-F is the "equidistant" line. F-B and F-D represent German claims. F-E-B depicts Danish claims, and F-E-D that of Netherlands.

the settlement of a dispute. The corrective power of the principle is extended to both procedural and substantive matters, which gives the exercise of it the appearance of a quasi-legislative function; something more than the application of strict law is warranted in certain cases.

The power of the Court to apply equity is given in Article 38 (2) of the Statute of the Court, which states that prior provisions of the Article "shall not prejudice the court to decide a case *ex aequo et bono* [according to what is right and good], if the parties agree thereto." One might mischievously imagine that this power opens the door to arbitrary use of judicial authority or discretion. However tribunals vested with such power are obligated to find grounds for decision based on legal analogies that conform to principles of law and justice—a mixture of righteousness and law that facilitates just settlements or compromises. One interesting case involving the application of the principle of equity is the *North Sea Continental Shelf Cases* (1969).

The case concerning the North Sea Continental Shelf involved the delineation of maritime boundaries for Germany, Denmark, and the Netherlands. Boundaries were to be delineated between Germany and Denmark, on the one hand, and Germany and the Netherlands on the other hand. The countries involved asked the Court to state the principles and rules of international law applicable to the delineation of areas of the North Sea Continental Shelf appertaining to each of them beyond what had already been established in the immediate vicinity of their coasts, and agreed to accept delineation based on the rules of the Court. The Court, then, was to set rules and the parties involved were to undertake negotiations.

The source of the dispute was disagreement over the prolongation of the partial coastal boundaries (see prolongation beyond the coastal boundaries in the adjoining map). Denmark and the Netherlands wanted the prolongation to be based on an "equidistance" principle, but the Federal Republic of Germany felt it would be deprived of its proper share of the continental shelf area if delimitation is not based on a principle of "proportionality" to the length of its North Sea coastline. The German proposal was supposed to guarantee "proportionality".

The "equidistance" principle dealt with the concavity and the convexity of the coastline involved, and sought justification from the 1958 Geneva Convention on the Continental Shelf, which was not ratified by Germany. The German coastline was largely concave; therefore, the outer limits of delimitation based on the "equidistance" principle did not make it feasible for Germany to gain equal share or access to the North Sea continental shelf. This was not the case for Denmark and the Netherlands. Was the German predicament "a special circumstance"? Article 6 (2) of the Geneva Convention on the Continental Shelf (1958) states the following:

> Where the same continental shelf is adjacent to the territories of two adjacent States, the boundary of the continental shelf shall be determined by agreement between them. In the absence of agreement, and unless another boundary

> line is justified by special circumstances, the boundary shall be determined by the application of the principle of equidistance from the nearest points of the baselines from which the breadth of the territorial sea of each State is measured.

Denmark and the Netherlands saw no basis for special circumstances in the coastal configuration of Germany. The Germans, on the other hand, believed that the correct rule in such circumstances as those involving the North Sea Continental Shelf should be "just and equitable share" of the available continental shelf. Therefore, each of the states concerned was entitled to a continental shelf area extending up to the central point of the sea or, at least, extending to its median line. Alternatively, Germany claimed that if the "equidistance" principle is to be used, the configuration constituted a special circumstance for a departure from the traditional method of delineation.[114]

Issues arising from the case included the following: (i) what is the right of a coastal state in respect to the continental shelf by virtue of sovereignty over land; (ii) are the provisions of a treaty binding on a state which has not ratified it; (iii) should the notion of natural prolongation supersede that of the principle of "equidistance"; and (iv) was the "equidistance" principle a rule of customary international law?

The Court stated, first, that the parties were under no obligation to apply the "equidistance" principle under the 1958 Convention or customary international law. The International Law Commission did not propose "equidistance" principle, as emerging customary international law and state practice had been insufficient for the principle to be characterized as customary. Therefore, the Convention was not in its origins declaratory of a mandatory rule of customary international law. It was, therefore, unnecessary to determine special circumstances.

Second, the doctrine of "just and equitable share" was at variance with the rights of coastal states to exercise sovereignty over land, i.e., natural prolongation of their land territory under sea, which *exists ipso facto* and *ab initio*. The right to exercise control over such land is inherent; therefore, no legal rights have to be performed.[115]

Third, the notion of the natural prolongation of land was to supersede the principle of "equidistance", in the sense that submarine areas are *ipso jure* entitlements of States, as prolongation of land territory under sea. As such, the "equidistance" principle could cause areas of natural prolongation of one State to be attributed to another State.

Fourth, that the application of the Geneva Convention required agreement through negotiation with tolerance or readiness to modify a chosen position on the issues. The parties were obligated to act in such a way that takes all circumstances into account—general configuration of the coasts of the parties, natural resources of the continental shelf, and proportionality of access to continental shelf, actual or prospective in the same region.

Fifth, that it based its decision on *ex aequo et bono*, a rule of law that called for the application of equitable principles, where the "equidistance" method could unquestionably lead to inequity.

Use of Writers in Judicial Settlement

Writers provide a source of reference to international law not just because they are writers, but because their discussions of cases provide convincing conclusions on rules of law—what Weston et al. consider to be an accurate and objective restatement of law rather than judicial opinions.[116] Article 38(d) of the Statute of the ICJ makes reference to specific publicists, "the teachings of the most highly qualified publicists of the various nations..." The relevance of writers depends on the amount of cases that could be assembled to justify their positions on rules of law. D'Amato sees these publicists, in a sense, as judges who do extensive research into several cases, correspondence, and newspaper reports in order to consistently establish a rule for extended judicial opinion.[117]

In *Queen v. Keyn* (1876), the Court of Crown Cases Reserved (CCCR), alluded to writers as a source of international law.[118] In 1876 a German ship collided with an English vessel less than three miles from Dover Beach. The German captain was, thereafter, accused of manslaughter.

The central issue in the case became whether the CCCR had jurisdiction over foreigners within the three-mile range. The Chief Justice, Cockburn, ruled that in the absence of statutory provisions, the court had no jurisdiction over foreigners. This was a shift to emphasize municipal law transforming international law (transformation) rather than incorporation. The majority of the Court (7-6) relied on writers in the absence of a statute.

The writings of the publicists were far less unanimous and at best ambiguous. For which the Chief Justice observed that regardless of how labor intensive the writings of the publicists are in ascertaining or elucidating the principles and rules of law, they cannot make a law. The publicists could only make a law after their writings have received the approval and consent/assent of the nations to be bound by it. The assent may manifest itself in treaty, and acknowledge concurrence of governments, or through established usage.

The importance of publicists, therefore, rests not in the expression of judicial opinions but in their reference to facts through the utilization of treaties and usage. For example, established usage shows that merchant vessels on the high seas are held to be subject only to the law of the nation under whose flag they sail. When they are in the ports of foreign nations they have dual obligation, for they are subject to municipal and international law.

The problem with odious debt is that it has been of comparative recency (a twentieth century phenomenon) with very little authoritative writing on it. In addition, although judicial settlement is an avenue that is open to the settlement of disputes between and among states involving odious debts, the International Court, with the exception of the Polish case (1919) that involved treaty interpretation, has not been used for such cases to establish a judicial tradition. Indeed in the absence of a treaty, it is one of those forums which would adequately give the issue of odiousness finality in international law. It is not likely that states would explore this possibility in the short-run or in the near future because of the very nature of debt contracts and the agents involved. Issues concerning debt resolutions are normally provided for in contracts under arbitration rather than judicial settlements. African states are therefore not normally provided this option and they need not be enthusiastic about exploring it just now for reasons already mentioned. The best hope for these nations in the absence of the required political leadership would ultimately be found in treaty provisions.

Focus Questions

1. What is international law? Is there a role for international law in solving or preventing the African debt crisis? Why?
2. Are the African debts odious? What factors are responsible for the odiousness of the debts if they are? If not, why not (you may use your own interpretation of the 1919 treaty of Versailles concerning Polish debts and/or the Tinoco conflict)?
3. Why would a judicial settlement of the issue of odiousness be preferable to arbitration or resolution by a tribunal?
4. Explain how a multilateral convention against corruption can foster African economic development. Why are nations reluctant to fight corruption in real life?
5. What principles of law can the ICJ use to resolve international disputes involving hateful debts? Why is the prospect of using the ICJ to resolve debt conflicts far-fetched?
6. How does the requirement of a Poverty Reduction Strategy Paper (PRSP) for the disbursement of multilateral loans challenge the concept of odiousness?
7. Neither the arbitrary repudiation of debts, nor judicial settlements can make the poor countries better off. Do you agree? Why?
8. Why do you think equity and proportionality should or should not play a vital role in resolving or restructuring the African debts?

Epilogue

African underdevelopment is the result of an evolution of problems inherited from colonialism that were subsequently made worse by the new African élites in the post-colonial period. The new African élites who emerged as inheritors of the post-colonial states proved to be inept to deal with the problems they inherited. The political problems which cascaded out of the reach of the Europeans and Africans were largely associated with the reconfiguration of African societies, and the loss of those social values of political accountability, distributive justice, and checks on arbitrary political power; those social mores which defined the essence of a state or society.

These values are generic and consistent with the fundamental principles of what is considered international law today. From the *Oyo Mesi* to the *Poro* or the *Leopard-Skin* Chief, various African societies in what is sometimes regarded as "primitive" formations, manifested a fundamental sense of reverence for elders and respect for their kinsmen. Respect for political leadership was largely based on a sense of some divine obligation that was perceived as mutual, and the belief that all had a stake in what was considered to be a state or society. The dangers of wars were real and known. Knowledge of the adverse consequences of wars limited the scale of wars to avoid its internecine consequences. Wars were predominantly limited to access to trade routes, the enforcement of fines and the incorporation of neighboring territories when necessary. Captives of war became slaves, *servi*, and functioned as such with a potential for upward mobility.

The Berlin Conference (1884/5) was a symptom of a larger and looming problem on the horizon. What seemed to be the initial wisdom of British imperialism was to keep traditional culture intact, but colonialism was not designed to coexist with traditional values. Adjustments had to be made and cultural beliefs had to be casualties in the process. Economic necessity challenged the fundamental reasoning of colonialism. For example, taxing houses was an alien concept to the Africans. Reaching the Africans required middlemen. The African societies were already bonded to their chiefly political leaders, and the balkanization or unification of territories with disparate cultural backgrounds muddied the basis for any sense of nationalism or political advancement. In Sierra Leone, this contributed to the Hut Tax War of 1898; the call for secession; and the deep-seated cultural animosities. In the Sudan, after more than forty years of independence, the puzzle is yet to be solved.

The French were even more aggressive in the promotion of their culture, which they also felt could exist with the idea of imperialism. The policy of assimilation was a revolutionary and ambitious proposition. The French were able to reverse themselves in a timely manner to implement policies that were akin to the British paradigm. As if the objectives of imperialism were not adverse enough, Leopold II of Belgium gave it the ultimate rapacious outlook. Colonialism was not intended to give the indigenous Africans a significant or substantial amount of political participation, though debates of eventual withdrawal, at least among the British, dated back to the 1850s. It could be recalled that Disraeli had remarked that the "wretched colonies" would be independent in a few years.

In the British and French colonies, some Africans were already well educated, but they were granted no significant role in politics until much later in the imperial process. More worrisome was the fact that the ill-educated masses of the rural areas were all of a sudden expected to participate in a political process for which they had very little or no understanding. This opened the door for fractious politics and ruinous political alliances that were based on ethnic loyalty and regionalism.

The struggle for independence ensued with monstrous problems that the African élites claimed to understand and promised to resolve. The African political opportunists, who were in the midst of agitators for independence, were quick to show their ineptitude. They failed to construct plans for political unification and development, but they promptly struggled over the spoils of power for personal glory and economic enrichment. At the center of the struggle was the control over natural resources and the prolongation of political power, which was often manipulated by constitutional changes. This aberration of a typical democratic process necessitated a justification of their political ideology in convincing terms. They found justification in socialism or neo-imperialism; both of which were ostensible and worthless concepts for any meaningful development in the face of their assault on their citizens and natural resources.

Successful despotism depended on the use of the military or a well integrated civil-military relationship. Civil-military relations jeopardized the chances of success for nascent African republics. The Africanization of the military was conducted with deep ethnic prudence to safeguard the loyalty of the military to corrupt civilian administrations. Ever so often, rogues fell apart and the military interjected itself into civilian politics either to protect corrupt civilian administrations or to replace them. Military intervention in civilian politics has become a familiar sight in African politics; not so much to fix the problems associated with bad governance, but with very rare exceptions, to exacerbate it.

The alliance of the military with corrupt regimes, or the inability of the military to get politics right, rapidly fostered the conditions for African underdevelopment. Apart from the billions of foreign currencies that have been squandered by the African political leadership, it has been deemed necessary to spend extravagantly on defense to fend off opponents, appease the military personnel, or repel prospective foreign invasions. These policies of profligate spending and fraud compounded by wars and exogenous crises (like the oil crises) have prevented various African governments from significantly fulfilling obligations to social spending. The consequences are a *fait accompli,* underdevelopment.

The supposedly cash-starved governments looked to the international community for the provision of reckless loans and hateful debts. Highly liquid banks thought it fit to overindulge the African leaders in the disbursement of reckless loans which lent themselves to capital-flight, an increase in private assets and public debts. The consequences of bad debts are inimical to growth and development. For one thing, debt discourages not only domestic investment but also foreign investment, and wars scare off foreign investors. The absence of goal-oriented policies and the persistence of anarchy make living conditions intolerable.

While some Africans struggled for political power and designed methods to defraud their nations, some of the East Asian countries were mapping out long-term developmental goals. In a systematic manner, Singapore, for example, addressed the issues of nationalism, population growth, corruption, investment in human capital, export promotion, and competition in the global economy. For the past three decades Singapore has been registering comparatively substantial growth and development. The economic performance of Singapore is remarkable because of its comparative lack of natural resources in comparison to most African states. The glaring evidence of mismanagement in Africa has been the ocular polarization of the wealthy few and poverty of the majority.

The poor are left to survive with odds stacked against them with little hope of redemption. They understandably try to subsist and survive based on whatever they could get from their immediate environment. The pressure on the environment jeopardizes the chances of sustainable development. Trees are being slashed and burnt to promote subsistence farming, animals are hunted for cash, and there has been a growing incidence of migration from decrepit rural areas to the urban areas. The ill-equipped governments have a hard time dealing with population densities in urban areas. Poor sanitary conditions and assorted pollution become logical outgrowth of such migration. In the quandary of poverty, defalcation, and mismanagement, Africans must now deal with the AIDS epidemic, which is now decimating the African population. Much more international assistance is now inevitable for the continent to be rescued.

Apart from the much more topical issue of sustainable development, heavily indebted and poor countries are now faced with hateful debts which hung over subsequent generations. It is certain that the loans that aided flight capital have not benefited the states which are still severely underdeveloped. This makes the connection between loans and development or national benefit, far-fetched. The reversal of international complicity with hateful debts is slow and tardy. International creditors have tried to get around the issue of odiousness by linking loans to a commitment to reduce poverty. This necessitates the provision of a poverty reduction strategy paper (PRSP), for heavily indebted and poor nations seeking multilateral loans.

Odious debts imply culpability, the determination of which could be ascertained by the application of international law. International law has not provided a clear indication of odiousness by custom or judicial settlement. The Tinoco Arbitration argues against the arbitrary repudiation of debts because of the continuity of a state and the persistence of inherited obligation. With the exception of a few cases of repudiation, it has not been a general practice of nations to accept repudiation of sovereign debt as a principle or widely held practice. Customary international law cannot be of much help.

The greatest role for international law in dealing with odiousness lies in the signing and ratification of bilateral treaties or multilateral treaties dealing with corruption, international money laundering, confiscation, and restitution or repatriation. There is no doubt in international law that nations are obligated to respect treaties which they have ratified. Ratification of such a treaty will do less to reverse the consequences of the debt burden already evident, but it would certainly do more to forestall hateful debts.

Heavily indebted nations cannot feasibly look forward to international law for redemption in the absence of a treaty. They cannot also repudiate their debts easily and arbitrarily, or look to judicial settlement. These nations are too poor to finance their development on a sustained basis without external assistance or continued access to financial institutions. The successful amelioration of the African debt crisis depends more on negotiated settlements involving equity and state capacity to pay rather than international law or judicial settlement. Customary international law is not well developed and is fraught with problems of its own, especially the equality of states. Should non-participating states be governed by a custom? In the interest of global development, it is definitely prudent to revisit the African debt situation to meet much more practical sustainable standards that would not compromise the much needed social programs or investment for development.

Can Africa develop tomorrow? The key to African development is contingent on the political culture that would replace the demoded forms of sectionalism, corruption, and oppressive regimes. It is clearly not dependent on which economic theory is adopted just now, but what political structure and institutions would foster growth and development through accountability or benevolence, in short, growth and development in the correct political climate. Informed political participation is essential to filling the void which had existed since independence, because civic responsibility is indispensable to the developmental process; lost decades of nationalism or national interests makes this a challenging proposition.

Apart from eschewing and preventing widespread corruption, the social planner of the future has to focus on both political decentralization and distributive justice for fuller participation and societal ownership of government at regional levels to foster regional development and attenuate the harmful effects of ethnic loyalties.

The underdeveloped countries of Africa currently lack the capacity to sustain development in its weak or strong form. They therefore need a lot of help to amass human and physical capital to utilize the right technology in production. Urgent help is also needed to safeguard the continent against the AIDS epidemic, the provision of sanitary conditions, and saving the environment. The future of the poor African countries is not only dependent on what policies and attitudes the African rulers are going to adopt after more than three decades of failed policies, but how much the international community is willing to invest in developing and sustaining the right (correct) political institutions and economic relations. Nations generally accrue income through trade or exchange. Ensuring an increase in trade and income is one way to reduce reliance on foreign loans, which is much of a nuisance for creditors and African debtors alike. This would involve the capacity of the poor African nations to achieve considerable diversification in their articles of trade. The interaction of good politics and economics is obviously an indispensable requirement for African development in the future.

Notes

Introduction

1. Anthropologists generally classify pre-colonial African societies into state and stateless societies. State societies were generally well organized, with well-defined structure, functions and authority. They had well defined rules and an ambition to expand territorial frontiers. There has not been a comprehensive definition of the stateless, but it would be anachronistic or misleading to define such societies as anarchic. On the contrary, they have been classified based on political authority or social or political organization. Examples normally include the Bushmen, *Pygmies* and Neur of Southern Sudan. In the Stateless societies, informal institutions perform legislative and executive functions through informal meetings and secret societies. Also see Collins et al. eds. *Problems in African History* (New Jersey: Markus Wiener Publishers) 167-173.

2. Islamic religious wars are objectionably perceived of as a *jihad* in some circles, otherwise they are seen as a struggle to defend the Islamic faith.

Chapter 1. The Old Perception of State and Society in Africa

3. A man's sister's son (nephew) will be given preference for the inheritance of office and property. This practice was common among some groups of West Africa, including the *Sherbro* of Sierra Leone.

4. See http://www.onwar.com/aced/data/oscar/oyo1817.htm

5. See http://www.manigua.org/resources/orishas/yoruba_kings.html.

6 . Harris, Joseph. *Africans and Their History* (Ontario: Penguin Books Canada, 1987) 121.

7. See Harris, op.cit, p. 122

8. Foray, Cyril. *Historical Dictionary of Sierra Leone* (New Jersey & London: The Scarecrow Press, 1977) 123.

9. Kup, Alexander. *Sierra Leone: A Concise History* (North Vancouver BC: Douglas David & Charles, 1975) 41.

10. Newton, John. *Thoughts Upon the African Slave Trade* (London, 1787) 25-6

11. Newton, Ibid.

12. Little, Kenneth. *The Mende of Sierra Leone* (New York: Routledge & Kegan Paul, 1967) 29.

13. Little, op. cit., p.181.

14. See Http://philtar.ucsm.ac.uk/encyclopedia/sub/nuer.html.

15. Evans-Pritchard, Edward. *The Nuer: A Description of the Modes of Livelihood and Political Institutions of a Nilotic People* (Oxford University Press, 1940) 50-59.

16. Howell, Peter. *A Manual of Nuer Law* (London: Oxford University Press, 1954) 22-25.

17. Howell, op.cit., p.25.

18. Evans-Pritchard, op.cit., p.150.

19. Evans-Pritchard, Ibid.

20. Evans-Pritchard, op. cit., p.172.

21. The traditional way of life of the *Pygmies* has been radically altered over the years as a result of government regulation, particularly those which have restricted the hunting capacities of the *Pygmies*.

Chapter 2. Building The New African States

22. By 1914, the conference participants had fully divided Africa among themselves into fifty countries. Great Britain desired a Cape-to-Cairo collection of colonies and almost succeeded through their control of Egypt, Sudan (Anglo-Egyptian Sudan), Uganda, Kenya (British East Africa), South Africa, and Zambia, Zimbabwe, and Botswana (Rhodesia). The British also controlled Nigeria and Ghana (Gold Coast). France took much of western Africa, from Mauritania to Chad (French West Africa) and Gabon and the Republic of Congo (French Equatorial Africa). Belgium and King Leopold II controlled the Democratic Republic of Congo (Belgian Congo). Portugal took Mozambique in the east and Angola in the west. Italy's holdings were Somalia (Italian Somaliland) and a portion of Ethiopia. Germany took Namibia (German Southwest Africa) and Tanzania (German East Africa). Spain claimed the smallest territory - Equatorial Guinea (Rio Muni)". See de Blij, H.J. and Peter O. Muller *Geography: Realms, Regions, and Concepts*. The territorial awards ignored French claims to parts of the Congo and of Nigeria and the historical claim of Portugal to the mouth of the Congo

23. Fyfe, Christopher. *A history of Sierra Leone* (London: Oxford University Press, 1962) 488.

24. *Creole* is not used here to define the status of native immigrants in the colony or those who generally accepted western values.

25 The climatic condition in Nova Scotia was less hospitable for the Nova Scotians and promises of land and other comforts after the war were yet to be fulfilled. Through Thomas Peters, one of their numbers, they petitioned the British Crown to be resettled in Sierra Leone.

26. Fyfe, Christopher, op.cit., p.543.

27. Fyfe, Christopher, op.cit., p.566

28. Fyfe, Christopher, op.cit., p.549. Sir Samuel Lewis was the first African to be knighted. In 1894 he acted as chief Justice, and Queens Advocate in 1895.

29. Kup, Alexander, op. cit., p. 200.

30. *The Sierra Leone Weekly News*, March 12, 1921. Cited in Foray, Cyril, op.cit., p.161.

31. The members of the Executive Council included the Governor, the Chief Justice, the Queen's Advocate, the Colonial Secretary, and the officer commanding the troops. The Legislative Council consisted of the Executive Council and a number of members (about four in 1863) appointed by the Governor and approved by the secretary of state. Foray observes that the Governor was instructed to take into consideration "the wishes of the more intelligent portion of the community." Foray, Cyril, op. cit., p.16.

32. Foray Cyril, op.cit., p. 199.

33. All People's Congress (APC). *The Rising Sun* (London: IMPADS, 1982) 45.

34. cited in http://www.fordham.edu/halsall/mod/1884ferry.html.

35. Crowder, Michael. *West Africa Under Colonial Rule* (London: Hutchinson & Company, 1968) 72.

36. Fyle, M. *Introduction To The History of African Civilization Vol. II Colonial and Post-Colonial Africa* (Maryland: University Press of America, 1999) 29.

37. Ibid.
38. Thomson, David. *Europe Since Napoleon* (New York: McGraw-Hill, 1990) 457.
39. Fyle, Magbaily op.cit., p.32.
40. Ibid.

Chapter 3. Colonialism or Policy?

41. Ellis, Jane and Dawson Waldron. "Globalisation, Corruption and Poverty Reduction," *Development Bulletin,* 55 (July 2001):26.
42. Cox, Thomas. *Civil-Military Relations in Sierra Leone* (Massachusetts: Harvard University Press, 1976) 60.
43. Stevens, Siaka. *What Life Has Taught Me* (London: Kensal Press, 1984)235. "Baybayraybay" is a vernacular for large quantities.
44. Cox, Thomas, op. cit., p.61.
45. See Tables 3-7.
46. All People's Congress, op. cit., pp.143-144.
47. See http://encarta.msn.com/encyclopedia_761578969/Mobutu_Sese_Seko.html.
48. See http://lcweb2.loc.gov/cgi-bin/query/r?frd/cstdy:@field(DOCID+sg0033). Singapore as Part of Malaysia.
49. Ibid. (Singapore under Lee Kuan Yew).
50. See table 3.2.
51. Cardoso, Eliana and Ann Helwege. *Latin America's Economy* (Massachusetts: The MIT Press, 1995) 10.
52. World Bank. *The East Asian Miracle* (New York: Oxford University Press,1993) 22.
53. Op. cit. p. 2.
54. First under the leadership of Lee Kuan Yew, who resigned as Prime Minister on 28 November 1990 after 31 years in power, and immediately thereafter, Goh Chok Tong who became the second Prime Minister.

Chapter 4. Crises and underdevelopment in Africa

55. Diversification measure is based on the share of: manufacturing in GDP, and labor in industry; per capita energy commercial energy consumption; and merchandise export concentration index given by United Nations Conference on Trade and Development (UNCTAD). These countries normally have population of less than 75 million.
56. See World Development Report 2000/2001, p.3
57. "Incidence" is generally a word with distributive connotation resulting from program(s) or policies. The $1 or $2 a day categorization is closely associated with this concept.
58. Landes, David. "Why Are We So Rich and They So Poor?" *American Economic Association Papers and Proceedings* 80, no.2 (May 1989):1-13.
59.The Republic of Congo appeared in the list much later compared to the other three countries which appeared in 1980.
60.See Human Development Report 2000, p. 82 UNDP.
61. See Agénor Pierre-Richard and Peter Montiel. *Development Macroeconomics* (New Jersey: Princeton University Press, 1999) 573-574.

62. Extension is from Singer and Small (1994), and Licklider (1995).
63. Institute of Security Studies (ISS) estimates.
64. Ibid.
65. Central Intelligence Agency's (CIA) *World Fact Book.*
66. See ISS and CIA estimates.
67. Estimates are from the US Committee for Refugees.
68. See Http://www.ppu.org.uk/war/countries/africa/africa_index.html.
69. World Health Organization (WHO) estimates.
70. British Broadcasting Corporation (BBC) report on poverty level, 22 September, 2003.
71. CIA World Factbook (2003).
72. US Committee for Refugees (2004).
73. Mineral resources include: cobalt, copper, cadmium, petroleum, diamonds, gold, silver, zinc, manganese, tin, germanium, uranium, bauxite, iron ore, coal, timber, and coltan.
74. For measurement of sustainability see Hanley et al (2001) pp 140-141. (i) Green National Accounts—Green NNP = NNP- $(p_1 - mc_1)\Delta NR - (p_2 - mc_2)\Delta R - v(\Delta S)$. Where NNP= net national product (i.e. portion of income to be consumed without potential reduction in future consumption); p_1 and p_2 are prices of nonrenewable and renewable resources respectively; $mc_1(\Delta NR)$, $mc_2(\Delta R)$, and $v(\Delta S)$, are the marginal costs associated with changes in nonrenewable resources, renewable resources, and the abatement of pollution stock respectively. (ii) Genuine Savings (GS)= $S - \delta_m - \delta_n$; where S= Aggregate Savings, δ_m = depreciation of physical capital, and δ_n = depreciation of natural capital.
75. See US Census Bureau International Database.
76. Rostow proposes that in order to facilitate the "take-off" that a new elite, a new leadership, be created and given the scope to begin the construction of modern industrial society, a radical transformation of political power involving the change of men and model. See Rostow, Walt. *The Stages of Economic Growth: A Non-Communist Manifesto* (New York: Cambridge University Press, 1960) 7. See also Lombardi, Richard. *Debt Trap: Rethinking the Logic of Development* (New York: Praeger Publishers, 1985) 28-29.
77. See Http://www.uneptie.org/energy/publications/SEFI/energy-facts.pdf.
78. See Http://www.populationmedia.org/issues/demographics.html

Chapter 5. International Law and African Debt Burden

79. The three centuries separating Alexander the Great (d. 323 B.C.) and the formation of the Roman Empire (27 B.C.).
80. Rommen, Heinrich. *The Natural Law* (Indianapolis: Liberty Fund,1998) 20.
81. The *Code* was a collection that omitted repetition and inconsistencies, and statutes dealing with Roman religion. The *Digest* consisted of writings of Roman legal experts;the *Institutes* was a textbook on the basic principles of Roman law; and the *Novels*, a collection of new laws issued by Justinian between 534 and 565.
82. Rommen, Heinrich, op.cit., p. 27.
83. Rommen, Heinrich, op. cit., p. 67.
84. Walker, David, *The Oxford Companion of Law* (New York: Oxford University Press, 1989) 71.
85. Brierly, James, *The Law of Nations* (New York: Oxford University Press, 1963)1. Rules of international law are to be found in the ancient and medieval worlds because

man has always felt the necessity of rules since man started to be in political communities. As a branch of jurisprudence, international law is modern, dating back to the sixteenth century.

86. See *Greece v. United Kingdom*, 1924, PCIJ

87. See for example, the ongoing *Sierra Leone v. Charles Taylor* case. See also the General Assembly Resolution 260, December 1948 on Convention on The Prevention and Punishment of The Crime of Genocide.

88. Procedural matters in the council require seven votes including the concurring votes of the permanent members, and permanent members of the Council have a veto power on substantive matters.

89.Brierly, James, op.cit., p.41.

90. See Article 3, subsections (b) and (c) of the *Vienna Convention on The Law of Treaties* (1969).

91. It should be noted that oral commitments may be binding in international law. See the Ihlen Declaration.

92. A change of circumstance is not generally applicable to fundamental treaties of communal application, for example, the UN Charter. See Evans, Graham and Jeffrey Newnham. *The Penguin Dictionary of International Relations* (London: Penguin Books, 1998) 542-543.

93. See the *Charter of the United Nations and Statute of the International Court of Justice.*

94. See Reports of PCIJ, Series A, No.1, 17 August 1923.

95. Cited in Weston et. al. *International Law and World* Order (Minnesota: West Publishing Company, 1990) 80-81.

96. Ibid.

97. The Paquette Habana was captured by United States Gunboat Castine, and The Lola by United States steamship, Dolphin.

98. Cited in Brierly, James, op.cit., p.65.

99. See Weston et. al. op.cit., p.81.

100. See Brierly, James, op. cit., p.347.

101. See ICJ Statute Article 60.

102. See 13 U.S. 191 (1815). Adrian Bentzon v. Boyle and others (officers and crew of the privateer Comet).

103. Cited in 13 U.S. 191 (1815).

104. Chief Justice Marshall, building on the ruling of Sir William Scott in the *Jaffrow Catharina Case* in 1783 [13 U.S. 191,192], described land as "fixed." "Wherever the owner may reside, that land is hostile or friendly according to the condition of the country in which it is placed. It is no extravagant perversion of principle, nor is it a violent offence to the course of human opinion to say that the proprietor, so far as respects his interest in this land, partakes of its character; and that the produce, while the owner remains unchanged, is subject to the same disabilities."

105. This is the position taken by the architect of Article 38, Lord Phillimore.

106 See Cheng, bin, *General Principles of Law-As Applied by International Courts and Tribunals* (New York: Cambridge University Press, 1987) 23-25. "Civilized" was a word used to exclude from the application of the phrase, the systems of law utilized by primitive communities. Today the phrase, "general principles of law" has a much more global connotation. See Janis, mark. *An Introduction to International Law* (New York: Aspen Publishers,2003) 47.

107. Janis, Mark, Ibid.

108. See Weston et.al. op.cit., p.119.

109. See the Chorzow *Factory Case*, PCIJ, ser. A, No.9, p.31 (1927).

110. As a guarantee for the debt due to the Reich, the Treuhand obtained for the Reich a lien on all the shares of the OS. The Treuhand was to liquidate the purchase price exclusively by paying to the Reich the dividends on the shares of the OS although the Treuhand could pay part or all of the purchase price at any time to remove the lien on shares of nominal value corresponding to the payment made.

111. A similar action and withdrawal was made by the Bayerische between 1925 and 1928 before the same tribunal with the objective of obtaining annual indemnity until the restitution of the factory was made to the OS and thereby the restoration of the management to the Bayerische.

112. See Article 40 of the Statute of the International Court for procedures to submit a case or complaint.

113. This question is intended to address the issue of *res judicata,* identity of subject matter or juridical personality. Judgment 7 maintains that "the Chorzow undertaking was not and had never been from the outset (contract of 1915) an enterprise of the Reich, that the Bayerische was the business concern which worked it."

114. See map for competing claims.

115. Upholding such rights was consistent with delimiting territories (based on what already appertains to a state's coastal area) than apportioning (what is to be established anew).

116. See Weston et.al. op. cit., p.131.

117. Cited in Weston et.al. op. cit. p.132

118. See Crown Case 2 Ex. D. 63, 202-204 (Cr. Cas. Res. 1876).

References

Adams, Patricia. *Odious Debts*, London & Toronto: Probe International, 1991.

Agénor, Pierre-Richard and Peter Montiel. *Development Macroeconomics*, New Jersey: Princeton University Press, 1999.

Agénor, Pierre-Richard. *The Economics of Adjustment and Growth*, New York: Academic Press, 2000.

All People's Congress Secretariat. *The Rising Sun*, London: IMPADS, 1982.

Baker, Pauline and John Ausink. "State Collapse and Ethnic Violence: Toward a Predictive Model," *Parameters*, xxvi, no.1 (Spring 1996): 19-31.

Belgian Congo Public Relations Office. *Belgian Congo, 1*, 1959.

Borensztein, Eduardo. "Debt Overhang, Credit Rationing and Investment," *Journal of Development Economics* 32, (1990): 315-335.

Bosworth, Barry and Susan Collins. "Capital Flows to Developing Economies: Implications for Savings and Investment," *Brookings Papers on Economic Activity 1*, (1999): 143-177.

Boyce, James and Léonce Ndikumana. 22 November, 2002. *Africa's Debt: Who Owes Whom?* Http://www.odiousdebts.org/odiousdebts/print.cfm?ContentID=7129. 15 June, 2004.

Brierly, James. *The Law of Nations*, New York: Oxford University Press, 1963.

British Broadcasting Corporation News. 31 March 2004. *Timeline: A Chronology of Key Events*. Http://news.bbc.co.uk/1/hi/world/africa/country_profiles/ 1072684.stm. 5 June, 2004.

Brown, Lester. 06 December, 2000. *HIV Epidemic Restructuring Africa's Population*. Http://www.globalpolicy.org/socecon/develop/africa/2000/10311b.htm. 19 May, 2004.

Bulow, Jeremy and Kenneth Rogoff. "Cleaning up Third World Debt Without Getting Taken to the Cleaners," *Journal of Economic Perspectives*, no.4, (Winter 1990): 31-42.

Busharizi, Paul. 05 July, 2002. *Africa Needs Green to Fight Pollution, Says UN.* Http://www.enn.com/news/wire-stories/2002/ 07/07052002/. reu_47735.asp. 11 June, 2004.

Congo Democratic Republic Mission to the UN. 2000. *Our History* Http://www.un.int/drcongo/history. 08 June, 2004.

Cardoso, Eliana and Ann Helwege. *Latin America's Economy*, Massachusetts: The MIT Press, 1995.

Central Intelligence Agency. 18 December, 2003. *The World Factbook.* Http://www.cia.gov/cia/publications/factbook/geos/sn.html. 25 April 2004Cheng, Bin. *General Principles of Law As Applied to International Courts and Tribunals*, New York: Cambridge University Press, 1987.

Cohen, Daniel. "Low Investment and Large LDC Debt in the 1980's," *The American Economic Review,* 83, (June 1993): 437-449.

Cohen, Daniel. "The HIPC Initiative: How Really Good Is It?" OECD Centre, (2000): 22.

Collins, Robert, James Burns, Kathleen Hasselbald and Erik Ching, eds. *Problems in African History*, New Jersey: Markus Wiener Publishers, 1992.

Cox, Thomas. *Civil-Military Relations in Sierra Leone: A Case Study of African Soldiers in Politics,* Massachusetts: Harvard University Press, 1976.

Crowder, Michael. *West Africa Under Colonial Rule*, London: Hutchinson & Company, 1968.

De Blij, Harm and Peter Muller. *Geography: Realms, Regions, and Concepts,* US: John Wiley & Sons, 1977.

Easterly, William. "How did Highly Indebted Poor Countries Become Highly Indebted? Washington DC: World Bank, (2001): 37.

Elbadawi, Ibrahim and Nicholas Sambanis. "Why Are There So Many Civil Wars in Africa? Understanding and Preventing Violent Conflict," *Journal of African Economics,*9, (December 2000): 244-269.

Ellis, Jane and Dawson Waldron. "Globalization, Corruption and Poverty Reduction," *Development Bulletin*, 55, (July 2001): 26-29.

Evans, Graham and Jeffrey Newnham. *The Penguin Dictionary of International*

Relations, London: Penguin Books, 1998.
Evans-Pritchard, Edward. *The Nuer,* London: Oxford University Press, 1940.

Falola, Toyin. *The History of Nigeria*, Connecticut: Greenwood Press, 1999.

Foray, Cyril. *Historical Dictionary of Sierra Leone*, New Jersey & London: The Scarecrow Press, 1977.

Frankel, Jeffrey and Assaf Razin. *Fiscal Policies and Growth in the World Economy*, Massachusetts: MIT Press, 1996.

Fraser, Alistair. 01 October, 2004. *Bad Greenhouse.* Http://www.ems.psu.edu/~fraser/BadGreenhouse.html. 3 October, 2004.

Fyfe, Christopher. *A History of Sierra Leone*, London: Oxford University Press, 1962.

Fyfe, Christopher. *Sierra Leone Inheritance*, London: Oxford University Press, 1964.

Fyle, Magbaily. *Introduction to The History of African Civilization vols. I and II,* Maryland: University Press of America, 1999.

Garristen de Vries, Margaret. *Balance of Payments Adjustment, 1945 to 1986*, Washington, DC: International Monetary Fund, 1988.

Gaubatz, Kurt and Kathleen Kane. 2004. *The Tinoco Arbitration.* Http://www.gwu.edu/~jaysmith/Tinoco.html. 03 October, 2004.

Gillis, Malcolm, Dwight Perkins, Michael Romer and Donald Snodgrass. *Economics of Development*, New York: W.W. Norton & Company, 2001.

Global Security.Org 19 May 2004. *Congo Civil War.* Http://www.globalsecurity.org/military/world/war/congo.htm. 9 June, 2004.

Halsall, Paul.01 July, 1998. *Modern History Sourcebook: Jules Ferry (1832-1893): On French Colonial Expansion.* Http://www.fordham.edu/ halsall/ mod/1884ferry.html. 10 May, 2004.

Hahn, Chinhee and Jong-il Kim. "Sources of East Asian Growth: Some Evidence from Cross-country Studies," *Korea Development Institute*, (1999): 44.

Hana, Mahmoud. "Central African Republic," *African Perspective*, 4, no.14

(2003):6.Http://www.sis.gov.eg/public/africanmag/issue14/ html/prof02.htm. 06 March, 2004.

Hanley, Nick, Jason Shogren and Ben White. *Introduction to Environmental Economics*, New York: Oxford University Press, 2001.

Harris, Joseph. *Africans and Their History*. Ontario: Penguin Books Canada, 1987.

Howell, Peter. *A Manual of Neur Law*. London: Oxford University Press, 1954.

Ibrahim, Youssef. 28 October, 1998. *AIDS Is Slashing Africa's Population, UN Survey Finds.*Http://www.artsci.wustl.edu/~anthro/courses/306/aids-un.html. 04 October, 2004.

International Monetary Fund (IMF). 01 September, 2004. *Debt Relief Under the Heavily Indebted Poor Countries (HIPC) Initiative: A Factsheet* Http://www.imf.org/external/np/hipc/hipc.htm. 30 September, 2004.

IMF. *Poverty Reduction and Debt Relief for Poor Countries, IMF Annual Report,* Washington DC: IMF, 2000.

IMF. 01 January, 2003. *Proposals for a sovereign Debt Restructuring Mechanism (SDRM)*. Http://www.imf.org/external/np/exr/facts/sdrm.htm. 17 June, 2004.

Janis, Mark. *An Introduction to International Law*, New York: Aspen Publishers, 2003.

Jechoutek, Karl. 2003. *Facts and Figures*. Http://www.uneptie.org/energy/ publications/SEFI/energy-facts.pdf. 04 May, 2004.

Khalfan Ashfaq, Jeff King and Bryan Thomas. "Advancing the Odious Debt Doctrine" Centre for International Sustainable Development Law, Canada: McGill University, 2002.

Krueger, Anne. *A new Approach to Sovereign Debt Restructuring*, Washington DC: International Monetary Fund, 2002.

Krugman, Paul. "Reducing Developing Country Debt," *Revista de Análisis Económico*, vol 4, no.2 (November 1989): 3-18.

Krugman, Paul. and Lance Taylor. "Contractionary Effects of Devaluation," *Journal of International Economics*, 8, (1978): 445-456.

Kup, Alexander. *Sierra Leone: A Concise History*, North Vancouver BC: Douglas David & Charles, 1975.

Landes, David. "Why Are we So Rich and They So Poor?" *American Economic Review,* 80, no.2 (May1989): 1-13.

Larsen, Janet. 2002. *Population Growing by 80 Million Annually.* Http://www.populationmedia.org/issues/demographics.html. 06 June, 2004.

Larsen, Janet. 23 January, 2003. *Population Growth Leading to Land Hunger.* Http://www.earth-policy.org/updates/Update21.htm. 11 June, 2004.

Library of Congress. 30 December, 1989. *Singapore: Toward New Leadership.* Http://lcweb2.loc.gov/cgi-bin/query2/r?frd/cstdy:@field(DOCID+sg0036.15 April, 2004.

Library of Congress. 30 December, 1989. *Singapore: Aftermath of War, 1945-55.*Http://lcweb2.loc.gov/cgi-bin/query2/r?frd/cstdy:@field(DOCID+sg0028. 15 April, 2004.

Library of Congress.30 December, 1989. *Singapore: Singapore as Part of Malaysia.* Http://lcweb2.loc.gov/cgi-bin/query2/ r?frd/cstdy:@field (DOCID+sg0033. 15 April, 2004.

Library of Congress. 30 December, 1989. *Singapore: Under Lee Kuan Yew.* Http://lcweb2.loc.gov/cgi-bin/query2/r?frd/cstdy:@field(DOCID+sg00365. 15 April, 2004.

Library of Congress. 30 December, 1989. *Singapore: Crown Colony, 1867-1918.* Http://lcweb2.loc.gov/cgi-bin/query2/r?frd/cstdy:@field (DOCID+sg0023. 15 April, 2004.

Licklider, Roy. "The Consequences of Negotiated Settlements in Civil Wars 1945-1993,"*American Political Science Review*, 89, no.3 (September 1995): 681-690

Little, Kenneth. *The Mende of Sierra Leone*, New York: Routledge & Kegan Paul, 1967.

Lombardi, Richard. *Debt Trap: Rethinking the Logic of Development*, New York: Praeger Publishers, 1985.

Marigua.org and Charly Barbara. 2002. *Yoruba Kings of the Second Oduduwa Dynasty.* Http://www.manigua.org/resources/orishas/yoruba_kings.html.

4 April, 2004.

Mankiw, Gregory, David Romer and David Weil. "A Contribution to the Empirics of Economic Growth," *The Quarterly Journal of Economics,* 107 (May 1992): 407-437.

Mcleod, Darryl. Fall 2003. *ECGA 5450: Stabilization Policy in Developing Countries*. Http://www.gdsnet.org/classes/ECGA5450.htm. 15 May, 2004.

Melicher, Ronald. and Edgar Norton. *Finance*, New Jersey: John Wiley and Sons, 2003.

Mussa, Michael and Miguel Savastano. "The IMF Approach to Economic Stabilization," *NBER*, 14 (1999): 79-128.

Moore, Mick. "Political Underdevelopment," *Institute of Development Studies* (2000): 34.

MSN Encarta. 2004. *Mobutu Sese Seko*. Http://encarta.msn.com/ encycopedia761578969/ mobutusesesekо.html. 12 May, 2004.

Mutume, Gumisai. "Whither the Debt?" *Africa Recovery*, 15, no.3 (October 2001):26.

National Aeronautics and Space Administration. 17 February, 2004. *Natural Hazards*. Http://earthobservatory.nasa.gov/NaturalHazards/ naturalhazardsv2.php3?imgid=11981. 11 June, 2004.

Ndikumana, Léonce and James Boyce. "Public Debts and Private Assets: Explaining Capital Flight from Sub-Saharan Countries," *World Development,* 31, no.31 (January 2003):107-130.

Newton, John. *Thoughts upon the African Slave Trade*, London, 1787.

Odious Debts.Org. 2002. *What are Odious Debts?* Http://www.odiousdebts.org/ odiousdebts/index.cfm?DSP=subcontent&AreaID=3. 12 June, 2004.

Onwar.com. 16 December, 2000. *Civil war in Oyo 1817-1835* Http://www.onwar.com/aced/data/oscar/oyo1817.htm. 4 April 2004.

Pattillo, Catherine, Luca Ricci, and Hélène Poirson. "External Debt and Growth," *IMF Working Paper*, WP/02/69 (2002):44.

Peace Pledge Union. 26 February, 2003 *Wars and armed Conflicts Since 1945-*

Africa.Http://www.ppu.org.uk/war/countries/africa/africa_index.html. 4 June, 2004.

People's Friendship University.2004. *Patrice Lumumba*. Http://www.sci.pfu.edu.ru/~asemenov/lumumba/lumumba.htm. 6 march, 2004.

Philtar. 2004. *Nuer Religion* Http://philtar.ucsm.ac.uk/ encyclopedia/ sub/nuer.html. 4 February, 2004.

Porter, Arthur. *Creoledom*, London: Oxford University Press, 1963.

Robbins, Richard. 28 April, 2003. "Anti-IMF/World Bank Protests in The Global South 1976-2001(a partial list)." *Global Problems and the Culture of Capitalism*. Http://faculty.plattsburgh.edu/richard.robbins/ legacy/AntiIMF%20protests%201976-2001.h. 11 June, 2004.

Rodney, Walter. *How Europe Underdeveloped Africa*, London & Tanzania: Bogle-L'Ouverture Publications, 1982.

Rogoff, Kenneth and Jeromin Zettelmeyer. "Bankruptcy Procedures for Sovereigns: A History of Ideas 1976-2001," *IMF Staff Papers*, 49, no.3 (2002): 470-500.

Rommen, Heinrich. *The Natural Law*, Indianapolis: Liberty Fund, 1998.

Rostow, Walt. *The Stages of Economic Growth: A Non-Communist Manifesto*, New York: Cambridge University Press, 1960.

Sachs, Jeffrey. "A Strategy for efficient Debt Reduction," *Journal of Economic Perspectives*, 4. no.1 (1990): 19-29.

Sachs, Jeffrey, Kwesi Botchwey, Maciej Cuchra and Sara Sievers. "Implementing Debt Relief for the HIPCs" *Center for International Development,* (August 1999):23.

Scaruffi, Piero. 2004. *Wars and Genocides of the 20'th Century*. Http://www.scaruffi.com/politics/massacre.html. 19 November, 2004.

Schneider, Benu. *Measuring Capital Flight: Estimates and Interpretations*, London: Overseas Development Institute, 2003

Shah, Anup. 16 July, 2003. *Causes of Poverty: Structural Adjustment—a major cause of poverty*. Http://www.globalissues.org/TradeRelated/sap.asp. 15

June, 2004.

Shah, Anup. 28 April, 2004. *Causes of Poverty*. Http://www.globalissues.org/TradeRelated/Facts.asp. 23 June, 2004.

Shah, Anup. 31 October, 2003. *Conflicts in Africa: The Democratic Republic of Congo*.Http://www.globalissues.org/geopolitics/Africa/DRC.asp?p=1. 11 June, 2004.

Shah, Anup. 30 August, 2001. *Debt Undermining Development: The Heavily Indebt Poor Countries Initiative is Not Working*. Http://www.globalissues.org/TradeRelated/Debt/HIPC.asp. 15 June, 2004.

Singer, David and Melvin Small. *Correlates of war Project: International and Civil War Data 1816-1992,* Michigan: ICPSR., 1994.

Stevens, Siaka. *What Life Has Taught Me*, London: Kensal Press, 1984.

Stewart, Frances and Valpy Fitzgerald. *War and Underdevelopment Vol.1*, New York: Oxford University Press, 2001.

Taylor, Lance. *Varieties of Stabilization Experience*, London: Clarendon Press, 1988.

Thomson, David. *Europe Since Napoleon*, New York: McGraw-Hill, 1990.

United Nations. *Charter of the United Nations and Statute of the International Court of Justice,* New York: United Nations, 1945.

United Nations. 2004. *United Nations Convention Against Corruption.* Http://www.unodc.org/unodc/en/crimeconventioncorruption.html?print=yes. 12 June, 2004.

United Nations. 8 April, 1983. *Vienna Convention on Succession of States in Respect of State Property, Archives and Debts*.Http://untreaty.un.org/ English/ sample/ EnglishInternetBible/partI/chapterIII/treaty12.asp. 17 June 2004.

United Nations. 2003. *World Population Prospects: The 2002 Revision Population Database*.Http://esa.un.org/unpp/assumptions.html. 12 June, 2004.

UNCTAD. *The Least Developed Countries Report,* Geneva: UN Conference on Trade and Development, 2004.

UNDP. *Human Development Report*, United Nations Development Program. 2000.

United Nations Foundation. 29 March, 2004. *Coup Attempt Fails in D.R.C. Capital; Mobutu Loyalists Suspected.* Http://www.unwire.org/UNWire/ 20040329/449_22267.asp. 18 June 2004.

US Census Bureau. 30 September 2004. *International Database.* Http://www.census.gov/ipc/www/idbnew.html. 03 October, 2004.

US Committee for Refugees. 2003. *World Refugee Survey 2003 Country Report* Http://www.refugees.org/world/countryrpt/africa/2003/ Congobrazaville.cfm. 20 June, 2004.

United States Environmental Protection Agency. 22 April, 2004. *Greenhouse Effect.* Http://www.epa.gov/globalwarming/kids/greenhouse.html. 13 June, 2004.

Walker, David. *Oxford Companion of Law*, New York: Oxford University Press, 1989.

Weston, Burns, Richard Falk and Anthony D'Amato. *Basic Documents In International Law and World Order*, Minnesota: West Publishing Company, 1990.

Weston Burns, Richard Falk and Anthony D'Amato. *International Law and World Order,* Minnesota: West Publishing, 1990.

Wikipedia. 22 September, 2004. *People's Action Party.*Http://en.wikipedia.org/ wiki/People's_Action_Party. 3 October, 2004.

Wilhelms, Saskia., "Foreign Direct Investment and Its Determinants in Emerging Economies," African Economic Policy Paper: Discussion Paper No.9 (July 1998):46.

Wilks, Ivor. *Asante in the Nineteenth Century,* London: Cambridge University Press, 1975.

World Bank. 2001. *Poverty in Sub-Saharan Africa: Issues and Recommendations.* Http://www.worldbank.org/afr/findings/ english/find74.htm 16 July, 2001.

World Bank. *World Development Report 2003: Sustainable Development in a Dynamic World,* New York: Oxford University Press, 2003.

World Bank. *World Development Report 2000/2001: Attacking Poverty,* New York: Oxford University Press, 2001.

World Bank. *World Development Indicator CD Rom*, 2003.

World Bank. 2004. *Financial Impact of The HIPC Initiative: First 24 country Cases*.Http://www.worldbank.org/hipc. 03 October, 2004.

World Bank. *The East Asian Miracle*, New York: Oxford University Press, 1993.

World Bank. 13 September, 2004. *What exactly is Inequality?* Http://www.worldbank.org/poverty/inequal/intro.htm. 04 October, 2004.

---1998. *Conflicts in the Sudan: A Failed State*.Http://www.mil.za/CSANDF/CJSupp/TrainingFormation/DefenceCollege/Researchpapers1998/conflict_in_the_sudan.htm.

--- *The Sierra Leone Weekly News*, Freetown: (12 March, 1921).

Index